MznLnx

Missing Links Exam Preps

Exam Prep for

Calculus: Early Transcendentals Version

Edwards & Penney, 6th Edition

The MznLnx Exam Prep is your link from the texbook and lecture to your exams.
The MznLnx Exam Preps are unauthorized and comprehensive reviews of your textbooks.

All material provided by MznLnx and Rico Publications (c) 2010
Textbook publishers and textbook authors do not particpate in or contribute to these reviews.

MznLnx

Rico
Publications

Exam Prep for Calculus: Early Transcendentals Version
6th Edition
Edwards & Penney

Publisher: Raymond Houge
Assistant Editor: Michael Rouger
Text and Cover Designer: Lisa Buckner
Marketing Manager: Sara Swagger
Project Manager, Editorial Production: Jerry Emerson
Art Director: Vernon Lowerui

Product Manager: Dave Mason
Editorial Assitant: Rachel Guzmanji
Pedagogy: Debra Long
Cover Image: Jim Reed/Getty Images
Text and Cover Printer: City Printing, Inc.
Compositor: Media Mix, Inc.

(c) 2010 Rico Publications
ALL RIGHTS RESERVED. No part of this work covered by the copyright may be reproduced or used in any form or by an means--graphic, electronic, or mechanical, including photocopying, recording, taping, Web distribution, information storage, and retrieval systems, or in any other manner--without the written permission of the publisher.

For more information about our products, contact us at:
Dave.Mason@RicoPublications.com

For permission to use material from this text or product, submit a request online to:
Dave.Mason@RicoPublications.com

Printed in the United States
ISBN:

Contents

CHAPTER 1
FUNCTIONS, GRAPHS, AND MODELS — 1

CHAPTER 2
PRELUDE TO CALCULUS — 15

CHAPTER 3
THE DERIVATIVE — 26

CHAPTER 4
ADDITIONAL APPLICATIONS OF THE DERIVATIVE — 39

CHAPTER 5
S THE INTEGRAL — 49

CHAPTER 6
APPLICATIONS OF THE INTEGRAL — 61

CHAPTER 7
TECHNIQUES OF INTEGRATION — 73

CHAPTER 8
DIFFERENTIAL EQUATIONS — 80

CHAPTER 9
POLAR COORDINATES AND PARAMETRIC CURVES — 93

CHAPTER 10
INFINITE SERIES — 102

CHAPTER 11
VECTORS, CURVES, AND SURFACES IN SPACE — 121

CHAPTER 12
PARTIAL DIFFERENTIATION — 136

CHAPTER 13
MULTIPLE INTEGRALS — 149

CHAPTER 14
VECTOR CALCULUS — 157

ANSWER KEY — 172

TO THE STUDENT

COMPREHENSIVE

The *MznLnx* Exam Prep series is designed to help you pass your exams. Editors at MznLnx review your textbooks and then prepare these practice exams to help you master the textbook material. Unlike study guides, workbooks, and practice tests provided by the texbook publisher and textbook authors, *MznLnx* gives you **all** of the material in each chapter in exam form, not just samples, so you can be sure to nail your exam.

MECHANICAL

The MznLnx Exam Prep series creates exams that will help you learn the subject matter as well as test you on your understanding. Each question is designed to help you master the concept. Just working through the exams, you gain an understanding of the subject--its a simple mechanical process that produces success.

INTEGRATED STUDY GUIDE AND REVIEW

MznLnx is not just a set of exams designed to test you, its also a comprehensive review of the subject content. Each exam question is also a review of the concept, making sure that you will get the answer correct without having to go to other sources of material. You learn as you go! Its the easiest way to pass an exam.

HUMOR

Studying can be tedious and dry. MznLnx's instructional design includes moderate humor within the exam questions on occassion, to break the tedium and revitalize the brain

Chapter 1. FUNCTIONS, GRAPHS, AND MODELS

1. In mathematics, the _____ is used to determine each point uniquely in a plane through two numbers, usually called the x-coordinate or abscissa and the y-coordinate or ordinate of the point. To define the coordinates, two perpendicular directed lines, are specified, as well as the unit length, which is marked off on the two axes Cartesian coordinate systems are also used in space and in higher dimensions.

   a. 15 theorem
   b. Cartesian coordinate system
   c. Coordinate
   d. Cylindrical coordinate system

2. Integration is an important concept in mathematics, specifically in the field of calculus and, more broadly, mathematical analysis. Given a function f of a real variable x and an interval [a, b] of the real line, the _____

$$\int_a^b f(x)\,dx,$$

is defined informally to be the net signed area of the region in the xy-plane bounded by the graph of f, the x-axis, and the vertical lines x = a and x = b.

The term '_____' may also refer to the notion of antiderivative, a function F whose derivative is the given function f.

   a. INTEGRAL
   b. Integral test for convergence
   c. Indefinite integral
   d. Integrand

3. In mathematics, the _____ (or replacement set) of a given function is the set of 'input' values for which the function is defined. For instance, the _____ of cosine would be all real numbers, while the _____ of the square root would be only numbers greater than or equal to 0 (ignoring complex numbers in both cases.) In a representation of a function in a xy Cartesian coordinate system, the _____ is represented on the x axis (or abscissa.)

   a. Domain
   b. BIBO stability
   c. BDDC
   d. 15 theorem

4. In mathematics, the _____ of a function is the set of all 'output' values produced by that function. Sometimes it is called the image, or more precisely, the image of the domain of the function. If a function is a surjection then its _____ is equal to its codomain.

   a. Piecewise-defined function
   b. Constant function
   c. Surjective
   d. Range

5. The terms '_____' and 'independent variable' are used in similar but subtly different ways in mathematics and statistics as part of the standard terminology in those subjects. They are used to distinguish between two types of quantities being considered, separating them into those available at the start of a process and those being created by it, where the latter (dependent variables) are dependent on the former (independent variables.)

In traditional calculus, a function is defined as a relation between two terms called variables because their values vary.

   a. BDDC
   b. BIBO stability
   c. 15 theorem
   d. Dependent variable

Chapter 1. FUNCTIONS, GRAPHS, AND MODELS

6. The terms 'dependent variable' and '_____' are used in similar but subtly different ways in mathematics and statistics as part of the standard terminology in those subjects. They are used to distinguish between two types of quantities being considered, separating them into those available at the start of a process and those being created by it, where the latter (dependent variables) are dependent on the former (independent variables.)

In traditional calculus, a function is defined as a relation between two terms called variables because their values vary.

- a. ACTRAN
- b. Independent variable
- c. AUSM
- d. ALGOR

7. In mathematics and computer science, the floor and ceiling functions map a real number to the next smallest or next largest integer. More precisely, floor(x) is the largest integer not greater than x and ceiling(x) is the smallest integer not less than x.

The _____ is also called the greatest integer or entier function, and the floor of a nonnegative x may be called the integral part or integral value of x. Computer languages (other than APL) commonly use ENTIER(x) (Algol), floor(x), or int(x) (C and C++).

- a. Floor function
- b. Multiplicative inverse
- c. Hyperbolic tangent
- d. Hyperbolic functions

8. In metric topology and related fields of mathematics, a set U is called _____ if, intuitively speaking, starting from any point x in U one can move by a small amount in any direction and still be in the set U. In other words, the distance between any point x in U and the edge of U is always greater than zero.

As an example, consider the _____ interval (0, 1) consisting of all real numbers x with 0 < x < 1. Here, the topology is the usual topology on the real line. We can look at this in two ways.

- a. AUSM
- b. ALGOR
- c. ACTRAN
- d. Open

9. In a totally ordered set all elements are mutually comparable, so such a set can have at most one minimal element and at most one maximal element. Then, due to mutual comparability, the minimal element will also be the least element and the maximal element will also be the greatest element. Thus in a totally ordered set we can simply use the terms minimum and _____.

- a. Racetrack principle
- b. Nth term
- c. Leibniz rule
- d. Maximum

10. In calculus, the _____ is a formula for the derivative of the composite of two functions.

In intuitive terms, if a variable, y, depends on a second variable, u, which in turn depends on a third variable, x, then the rate of change of y with respect to x can be computed as the rate of change of y with respect to u multiplied by the rate of change of u with respect to x. Schematically,

$$\frac{dy}{dx} = \frac{dy}{du} \cdot \frac{du}{dx}.$$

a. Differentiation rules
b. Product rule
c. Reciprocal Rule
d. Chain rule

11. A _____ officer is an officer of high military rank. The term or equivalent is used by nearly every country in the world. _____ can be used as a generic term for all grades of _____ officer, or it can specifically refer to a single rank that is just called _____.
a. BIBO stability
b. BDDC
c. 15 theorem
d. General

12. A _____ is an algebraic equation in which each term is either a constant or the product of a constant and (the first power of) a single variable. Linear equations can have one, two, three or more variables. Linear equations occur with great regularity in applied mathematics.
a. Quadratic formula
b. Cubic function
c. Quartic function
d. Linear equation

13. _____ is used to describe the steepness, incline, gradient, or grade of a straight line. A higher _____ value indicates a steeper incline. The _____ is defined as the ratio of the 'rise' divided by the 'run' between two points on a line, or in other words, the ratio of the altitude change to the horizontal distance between any two points on the line.
a. Y-intercept
b. 15 theorem
c. Slope
d. Sequence

14. In coordinate geometry, the _____ is the y-value of the point where the graph of a function or relation intercepts the y-axis of the coordinate system.

In other words, the _____ of a function is the y-value of the point at which it intersects the line x=0 (the y-axis.) Thus, if the function is specified in form y = f(x), the _____ is easy to find by calculating f.

a. 15 theorem
b. Y-intercept
c. Sequence
d. Slope

15. In physics, _____ is movement that changes the position of an object, as opposed to rotation. For example, according to Whittaker:

A _____ is the operation changing the positions of all points (x, y, z) of an object according to the formula

$$(x, y, z) \rightarrow (x + \Delta x, y + \Delta y, z + \Delta z)$$

where $(\Delta x, \Delta y, \Delta z)$ is the same vector for each point of the object. The _____ vector $(\Delta x, \Delta y, \Delta z)$ common to all points of the object describes a particular type of displacement of the object, usually called a linear displacement to distinguish it from displacements involving rotation, called angular displacements.

- a. BIBO stability
- b. BDDC
- c. Translation
- d. 15 theorem

16. In mathematics, the _____ (or modulus) of a real number is its numerical value without regard to its sign. So, for example, 3 is the _____ of both 3 and −3.

The _____ of a number a is denoted by $|a|$.

- a. ACTRAN
- b. Exponential function
- c. Area hyperbolic functions
- d. Absolute value

17. Continuous functions are of utmost importance in mathematics and applications. However, not all functions are continuous. If a function is not continuous at a point in its domain, one says that it has a _____ there. The set of all points of _____ of a function may be a discrete set, a dense set, or even the entire domain of the function.
- a. Vector
- b. BDDC
- c. 15 theorem
- d. Discontinuity

18. Cantor defined two kinds of _____ numbers, the ordinal numbers and the cardinal numbers. Ordinal numbers may be identified with well-ordered sets, or counting carried on to any stopping point, including points after an _____ number have already been counted. Generalizing finite and the ordinary _____ sequences which are maps from the positive integers leads to mappings from ordinal numbers, and transfinite sequences.
- a. ALGOR
- b. ACTRAN
- c. AUSM
- d. Infinite

19. In differential geometry there are a number of second-order, linear, elliptic differential operators bearing the name _____

The connection _____ is a differential operator acting on the various tensor bundles of a manifold, defined in terms of a Riemannian- or pseudo-Riemannian metric.

- a. Dirac operator
- b. Peetre theorem
- c. Semi-elliptic operator
- d. Laplacian

20. The _____ is a test to determine if a relation or its graph is a function or not. For a relation or graph to be a function, it can have at most a single y-value for each x-value. Thus, a vertical line drawn at any x-position on the graph of a function will intersect the graph at most once.
- a. BDDC
- b. 15 theorem
- c. BIBO stability
- d. Vertical line test

21. The _____ of any solid, liquid, plasma, vacuum or theoretical object is how much three-dimensional space it occupies, often quantified numerically. One-dimensional figures (such as lines) and two-dimensional shapes (such as squares) are assigned zero _____ in the three-dimensional space. _____ is commonly presented in units such as mL or cm³ (milliliters or cubic centimeters.)

   a. Vector potential
   b. Volume
   c. Klein-Gordon equation
   d. Dirac equation

22. A _____, in mathematics, is a polynomial function of the form $f(x) = ax^2 + bx + c$, where $a \neq 0$. The graph of a _____ is a parabola whose major axis is parallel to the y-axis.

The expression ax² + bx + c in the definition of a _____ is a polynomial of degree 2 or a 2nd degree polynomial, because the highest exponent of x is 2.

   a. Resultant
   b. Quadratic function
   c. Leading coefficient
   d. Discriminant

23. _____ is a type of motion in which the velocity of an object changes equal amounts in equal time periods. An example of an object having _____ would be a ball rolling down a ramp. The object picks up velocity as it goes down the ramp with equal changes in time.

   a. ACTRAN
   b. AUSM
   c. ALGOR
   d. Uniform Acceleration

24. In calculus, the _____ is a theorem regarding the limit of a function.

The _____ is a technical result which is very important in proofs in calculus and mathematical analysis. It is typically used to confirm the limit of a function via comparison with two other functions whose limits are known or easily computed.

   a. Table of limits
   b. Squeeze Theorem
   c. Limit of a sequence
   d. 15 theorem

25. Trigonometry is a branch of mathematics that deals with triangles, particularly those plane triangles in which one angle has 90 degrees (right triangles.) Trigonometry deals with relationships between the sides and the angles of triangles and with the _____ functions, which describe those relationships.

Trigonometry has applications in both pure mathematics and in applied mathematics, where it is essential in many branches of science and technology.

   a. Trigonometric functions
   b. Trigonometric integrals
   c. TRIGONOMETRIC
   d. Sine

26. In mathematics and its applications, a _____ system is a system for assigning an n-tuple of numbers or scalars to each point in an n-dimensional space. This concept is part of the theory of manifolds. 'Scalars' in many cases means real numbers, but, depending on context, can mean complex numbers or elements of some other commutative ring.

Chapter 1. FUNCTIONS, GRAPHS, AND MODELS

    a. Cylindrical coordinate system   b. 15 theorem
    c. Spherical coordinate system   d. Coordinate

27. The terms of the series are often produced according to a certain rule, such as by a formula, by an algorithm, by a sequence of measurements, or even by a random number generator. As there are an infinite number of terms, this notion is often called an _____. Unlike finite summations, series need tools from mathematical analysis to be fully understood and manipulated.
    a. Extreme value   b. Extreme Value Theorem
    c. Infinite series   d. Integration by substitution

28. In geometry, a _____ (pl. tori) is a surface of revolution generated by revolving a circle in three dimensional space about an axis coplanar with the circle, which does not touch the circle. Examples of tori include the surfaces of doughnuts and inner tubes.
    a. Hyperbolic paraboloid   b. Prolate
    c. Paraboloid   d. Torus

29. In the various subfields of physics, there exist two common usages of the term _____, both with rigorous mathematical frameworks.

- In the study of transport phenomena (heat transfer, mass transfer and fluid dynamics), _____ is defined as the amount that flows through a unit area per unit time. _____ in this definition is a vector.
- In the field of electromagnetism and mathematics, _____ is usually the integral of a vector quantity over a finite surface. The result of this integration is a scalar quantity. The magnetic _____ is thus the integral of the magnetic vector field B over a surface, and the electric _____ is defined similarly. Using this definition, the _____ of the Poynting vector over a specified surface is the rate at which electromagnetic energy flows through that surface. Confusingly, the Poynting vector is sometimes called the power _____, which is an example of the first usage of _____, above. It has units of watts per square metre (W·m^{-2})

One could argue, based on the work of James Clerk Maxwell, that the transport definition precedes the more recent way the term is used in electromagnetism. The specific quote from Maxwell is 'In the case of fluxes, we have to take the integral, over a surface, of the _____ through every element of the surface. The result of this operation is called the surface integral of the _____.

    a. BIBO stability   b. BDDC
    c. 15 theorem   d. Flux

30. In elementary mathematics, physics, and engineering, a _____ is a geometric object that has both a magnitude (or length), direction and sense, (i.e., orientation along the given direction.) A _____ is frequently represented by a line segment with a definite direction, or graphically as an arrow, connecting an initial point A with a terminal point B, and denoted by

            ⊠ ᵣ

The magnitude of the _____ is the length of the segment and the direction characterizes the displacement of B relative to A: how much one should move the point A to 'carry' it to the point B.

Chapter 1. FUNCTIONS, GRAPHS, AND MODELS

Many algebraic operations on real numbers have close analogues for vectors.

   a. 15 theorem
   c. BDDC
   b. Vector
   d. Linear partial differential operator

31. In mathematics a _____ is a construction in vector calculus which associates a vector to every point in a (locally) Euclidean space.

Vector fields are often used in physics to model, for example, the speed and direction of a moving fluid throughout space, or the strength and direction of some force, such as the magnetic or gravitational force, as it changes from point to point.

In the rigorous mathematical treatment, (tangent) vector fields are defined on manifolds as sections of a manifold's tangent bundle.

   a. 15 theorem
   c. Vector field
   b. BIBO stability
   d. BDDC

32. In physics, and more specifically kinematics, _____ is the change in velocity over time. Because velocity is a vector, it can change in two ways: a change in magnitude and/or a change in direction. In one dimension, _____ is the rate at which something speeds up or slows down.
   a. AUSM
   c. ALGOR
   b. ACTRAN
   d. Acceleration

33. In calculus, a branch of mathematics, the _____ is a measurement of how a function changes when its input changes. Loosely speaking, a _____ can be thought of as how much a quantity is changing at some given point. For example, the _____ of the position (or distance) of a vehicle with respect to time is the instantaneous velocity (respectively, instantaneous speed) at which the vehicle is traveling.

The process of finding a _____ is called differentiation. The fundamental theorem of calculus states that differentiation is the reverse process to integration.

   a. Stationary phase approximation
   c. Semi-differentiability
   b. Bounded function
   d. Derivative

34. A _____ is the curve defined by the path of a point on the edge of circular wheel as the wheel rolls along a straight line. It is an example of a roulette, a curve generated by a curve rolling on another curve.

The _____ is the solution to the brachistochrone problem (i.e. it is the curve of fastest descent under gravity) and the related tautochrone problem (i.e. the period of a ball rolling back and forth inside it does not depend on the ball's starting position.)

Chapter 1. FUNCTIONS, GRAPHS, AND MODELS

    a. Curtate cycloid
    c. Tractrix

    b. Prolate cycloid
    d. Cycloid

35. In geometry, the _____ (or simply the tangent) to a curve at a given point is the straight line that 'just touches' the curve at that point (in the sense explained more precisely below.) As it passes through the point of tangency, the _____ is 'going in the same direction' as the curve, and in this sense it is the best straight-line approximation to the curve at that point. The same definition applies to space curves and curves in n-dimensional Euclidean space.
    a. Lie derivative
    c. North pole

    b. Tangent line
    d. Minimal surface

36. In vector calculus, the _____ is an operator that measures the magnitude of a vector field's source or sink at a given point; the _____ of a vector field is a (signed) scalar. For example, consider air as it is heated or cooled. The relevant vector field for this example is the velocity of the moving air at a point.
    a. Gradient theorem
    c. Green's theorem

    b. Triple product
    d. Divergence

37. In vector calculus, the _____ of a scalar field is a vector field which points in the direction of the greatest rate of increase of the scalar field, and whose magnitude is the greatest rate of change.

A generalization of the _____ for functions on a Euclidean space which have values in another Euclidean space is the Jacobian. A further generalization for a function from one Banach space to another is the Fréchet derivative.

    a. Smooth function
    c. Lin-Tsien equation

    b. Symmetric derivative
    d. Gradient

38. In mathematics, the _____ states that every non-constant single-variable polynomial with complex coefficients has at least one complex root. Equivalently, the field of complex numbers is algebraically closed.

Sometimes, this theorem is stated as: every non-zero single-variable polynomial, with complex coefficients, has exactly as many complex roots as its degree, if each root is counted up to its multiplicity.

    a. Permutation
    c. Linear combinations

    b. 15 theorem
    d. Fundamental theorem of algebra

39. In physics, _____ is defined as the rate of change of position. it is vector physical quantity; both speed and direction are required to define it. In the SI (metric) system, it is measured in meters per second: (m/s) or ms^{-1}.
    a. BIBO stability
    c. Velocity

    b. BDDC
    d. 15 theorem

40. If a particular point on a sphere is (arbitrarily) designated as its _____, then the corresponding antipodal point is called the south pole and the equator is the great circle that is equidistant to them. Great circles through the two poles are called lines (or meridians) of longitude, and the line connecting the two poles is called the axis of rotation. Circles on the sphere that are parallel to the equator are lines of latitude.

a. Minimal surface
c. Sphere
b. Tangent line
d. North pole

41. In mathematics and elsewhere, the adjective _____ means 'fourth order', such as the function x^4. A _____ number is a number which equals the fourth power of an integer.
   a. Reduction
   b. BDDC
   c. Quartic
   d. 15 theorem

42. In mathematics, a _____ is any function which can be written as the ratio of two polynomial functions.

$$y = \frac{x^2 - 3x - 2}{x^2 - 4}$$

In the case of one variable, x, a _____ is a function of the form

$$f(x) = \frac{P(x)}{Q(x)}$$

where P and Q are polynomial function in x and Q is not the zero polynomial. The domain of f is the set of all points x for which the denominator Q(x) is not zero.

   a. 15 theorem
   b. BIBO stability
   c. BDDC
   d. Rational function

43. In mathematics, an _____ is informally a function which satisfies a polynomial equation whose coefficients are themselves polynomials. For example, an _____ in one variable x is a solution y for an equation

$$a_n(x)y^n + a_{n-1}(x)y^{n-1} + \cdots + a_0(x) = 0$$

where the coefficients $a_i(x)$ are polynomial functions of x. A function which is not algebraic is called a transcendental function.

   a. ACTRAN
   b. Algebraic function
   c. AUSM
   d. ALGOR

44. An _____ of a real-valued function y = f(x) is a curve which describes the behavior of f as either x or y tends to infinity.

In other words, as one moves along the graph of f(x) in some direction, the distance between it and the _____ eventually becomes smaller than any distance that one may specify.

a. ACTRAN
b. ALGOR
c. Asymptote
d. AUSM

45. In Geometry, the _____ is an algebraic curve defined by the equation

$$x^3 + y^3 - 3axy = 0.$$

It forms a loop in the first quadrant with a double point at the origin and asymptote

$$x + y + a = 0.$$

It is symmetrical about y = x.

a. Curve
b. Cochleoid
c. Folium of Descartes
d. Prolate cycloid

46. For the largest k where $a_k \neq 0$, a_k is called the _____ of P because most often, polynomials are written starting from the left with the largest power of x. So for example the _____ of the polynomial

$$4x^5 + x^3 + 2x^2$$

is 4.

The coefficients of polynomial also may be in the other order:

$$Q(x) = a_0 x^k + a_1 x^{k-1} + \cdots + a_{k-1} x^1 + a_k$$

and must be $a_0 \neq 0$ and a_0 is the _____ of Q.

a. Resultant
b. Symmetric function
c. Discriminant
d. Leading coefficient

47. _____ is how much exposed area an object has. It is expressed in square units. If an object has flat faces, its _____ can be calculated by adding together the areas of its faces.

a. Lipschitz domain
b. Vector area
c. Plane curve
d. Surface area

48. In mathematics, a _____ is a constant multiplicative factor of a certain object. For example, in the expression $9x^2$, the _____ of x^2 is 9.

The object can be such things as a variable, a vector, a function, etc.

Chapter 1. FUNCTIONS, GRAPHS, AND MODELS

    a. Binomial type
    c. Degree of the polynomial
    b. Resultant
    d. Coefficient

49. A _____ is perfectly round geometrical object in three-dimensional space, such as the shape of a round ball. Like a circle in two dimensions, a perfect _____ is completely symmetrical around its center, with all points on the surface lying the same distance r from the center point. This distance r is known as the radius of the _____.

    a. Tangent line
    c. Sphere
    b. North pole
    d. Minimal surface

50. A _____ is a differential equation that describes the conservative transport of some kind of quantity. Since mass, energy, momentum, and other natural quantities are conserved, a vast variety of physics may be described with continuity equations.

All the examples of continuity equations below express the same idea.

    a. BIBO stability
    c. 15 theorem
    b. Continuity equation
    d. BDDC

51. In mathematics, _____ and minima, known collectively as extrema, are the largest value (maximum) or smallest value (minimum), that a function takes in a point either within a given neighbourhood (local extremum) or on the function domain in its entirety (global extremum.)

Throughout, a point refers to an input (x), while a value refers to an output (y): one distinguishing between the maximum value and the point (or points) at which it occurs.

A real-valued function f defined on the real line is said to have a local maximum point at the point x^*, if there exists some $\varepsilon > 0$, such that $f(x^*) \geq f(x)$ when $|x - x^*| < \varepsilon$.

    a. Racetrack principle
    c. Related rates
    b. Leibniz formula
    d. Maxima

52. In mathematics, the _____ are functions of an angle. They are important in the study of triangles and modeling periodic phenomena, among many other applications. _____ are commonly defined as ratios of two sides of a right triangle containing the angle, and can equivalently be defined as the lengths of various line segments from a unit circle.

    a. Trigonometric integrals
    c. Trigonometric functions
    b. Trigonometric
    d. Sine integral

53. A _____, sometimes known as an energy shield, force shield typically made of energy or charged particles, that protects a person, area or object from attacks or intrusions.

A University of Washington in Seattle group has been experimenting with using a bubble of charged plasma to surround a spacecraft, contained by a fine mesh of superconducting wire. This would protect the spacecraft from interstellar radiation and some particles without needing physical shielding.

Chapter 1. FUNCTIONS, GRAPHS, AND MODELS

    a. Force field
    b. BIBO stability
    c. BDDC
    d. 15 theorem

54. The _____ is a function in mathematics. The application of this function to a value x is written as exp(x). Equivalently, this can be written in the form e^x, where e is a mathematical constant, the base of the natural logarithm, which equals approximately 2.718281828, and is also known as Euler's number.
    a. ACTRAN
    b. Area hyperbolic functions
    c. Integral part
    d. Exponential function

55. The function $\log_b(x)$ depends on both b and x, but the term _____ in standard usage refers to a function of the form $\log_b(x)$ in which the base b is fixed and so the only argument is x. Thus there is one _____ for each value of the base b (which must be positive and must differ from 1.) Viewed in this way, the base-b _____ is the inverse function of the exponential function b^x.
    a. BIBO stability
    b. BDDC
    c. 15 theorem
    d. Logarithm function

56. The _____, formerly known as the hyperbolic logarithm, is the logarithm to the base e, where e is an irrational constant approximately equal to 2.718281828. It is also sometimes referred to as the Napierian logarithm, although the original meaning of this term is slightly different. In simple terms, the _____ of a number x is the power to which e would have to be raised to equal x -- for example the natural log of e itself is 1 because e^1 = e, while the _____ of 1 would be 0, since e^0 = 1.
    a. Natural Logarithm
    b. 15 theorem
    c. BDDC
    d. BIBO stability

57. In infinitesimal calculus, a _____ is traditionally an infinitesimally small change in a variable. For example, if x is a variable, then a change in the value of x is often denoted Δx (or δx when this change is considered to be small.) The _____ dx represents such a change, but is infinitely small.
    a. Dirichlet integral
    b. The Method of Mechanical Theorems
    c. Local maximum
    d. Differential

58. _____, a field in mathematics, is the study of how functions change when their inputs change. The primary object of study in _____ is the derivative. A closely related notion is the differential.
    a. Slant asymptote
    b. Differential calculus
    c. Concave downwards
    d. Ramp function

59. The _____ specifies the relationship between the two central operations of calculus, differentiation and integration.

The first part of the theorem, sometimes called the first _____, shows that an indefinite integration can be reversed by a differentiation.

The second part, sometimes called the second _____, allows one to compute the definite integral of a function by using any one of its infinitely many antiderivatives.

a. Leibniz formula
c. Limits of integration
b. Periodic function
d. Fundamental theorem of calculus

60. In mathematics, a function f defined on some set X with real or complex values is a _____ function, if the set of its values is _____. In other words, there exists a number M>0 such that

$$|f(x)| \leq M$$

for all x in X.

Sometimes, if $f(x) \leq A$ for all x in X, then the function is said to be _____ above by A.

a. Stationary phase approximation
c. Bounded
b. Differential coefficient
d. Concave upwards

61. In mathematics, a real-valued function f defined on an interval (or on any convex subset of some vector space) is called convex, _____, concave up or convex cup, if for any two points x and y in its domain C and any t in [0,1], we have

$$f(tx + (1-t)y) \leq tf(x) + (1-t)f(y).$$

Convex function on an interval.

In other words, a function is convex if and only if its epigraph (the set of points lying on or above the graph) is a convex set.

Pictorially, a function is called 'convex' if the function lies below the straight line segment connecting two points, for any two points in the interval.

A function is called strictly convex if

$$f(tx + (1-t)y) < tf(x) + (1-t)f(y)$$

for any t in (0,1) and $x \neq y$.

A function f is said to be concave if − f is convex.

a. Concave upwards
c. Third derivative
b. Mountain pass theorem
d. Vertical asymptote

62. In mathematics, an _____, is the apparent shape of a circle viewed obliquely from outside it, as distinct from a hyperbola which is the shape seen from inside. It is the finite or bounded case of a conic section as a shape cut in a cone by a plane, the unbounded cases being the parabola, which like the _____ remains connected, and the hyperbola, which separates into two connected components or branches.

Equivalently an _____ can be defined as the locus of points, or path traced out, in a plane such that the sum of the distances from the moving point to two fixed points remains constant.

    a. ALGOR
    b. AUSM
    c. ACTRAN
    d. Ellipse

63. _____ is any physical or virtual entity that is owned by an individual or jointly by a group of individuals. An owner of _____ has the right to consume, sell, rent, mortgage, transfer and exchange his or her _____. Important widely-recognized types of _____ include real _____, personal _____ (other physical possessions), and intellectual _____ (rights over artistic creations, inventions, etc.), although the latter is not always as widely recognized or enforced.
    a. Property
    b. 15 theorem
    c. BIBO stability
    d. BDDC

64. In mathematics, a _____ is an ordered list of objects (or events). Like a set, it contains members (also called elements or terms), and the number of terms (possibly infinite) is called the length of the _____. Unlike a set, order matters, and the exact same elements can appear multiple times at different positions in the _____.
    a. 15 theorem
    b. Y-intercept
    c. Slope
    d. Sequence

Chapter 2. PRELUDE TO CALCULUS

1. An _____ is a type of quadric surface that is a higher dimensional analogue of an ellipse. The equation of a standard axis-aligned _____ body in an xyz-Cartesian coordinate system is

$$\frac{x^2}{a^2} + \frac{y^2}{b^2} + \frac{z^2}{c^2} = 1$$

where a and b are the equatorial radii (along the x and y axes) and c is the polar radius (along the z-axis), all of which are fixed positive real numbers determining the shape of the _____.

More generally, a not-necessarily-axis-aligned _____ is defined by the equation

$$\mathbf{x}^T A \mathbf{x} = 1$$

where A is a symmetric positive definite matrix and x is a vector.

    a. Ellipsoid   b. ALGOR
    c. AUSM   d. ACTRAN

2. In vector calculus a _____ is a vector field which is the gradient of a scalar potential. There are two closely related concepts: path independence and irrotational vector fields. Every _____ has zero curl (and is thus irrotational), and every _____ has the path independence property.

    a. Del   b. Divergence Theorem
    c. Conservative vector field   d. Green's theorem

3. In Geometry, the _____ is an algebraic curve defined by the equation

$$x^3 + y^3 - 3axy = 0$$

It forms a loop in the first quadrant with a double point at the origin and asymptote

$$x + y + a = 0$$

It is symmetrical about y = x.

    a. Folium of Descartes   b. Curve
    c. Cochleoid   d. Prolate cycloid

4. A _____ of a curve is a line that (locally) intersects two points on the curve. The word secant comes from the Latin secare, for to cut.

It can be used to approximate the tangent to a curve, at some point P. If the secant to a curve is defined by two points, P and Q, with P fixed and Q variable, as Q approaches P along the curve, the direction of the secant approaches that of the tangent at P, assuming there is just one.

a. Curve
b. Witch of Agnesi
c. Kappa curve
d. Secant line

5. In geometry, the _____ (or simply the tangent) to a curve at a given point is the straight line that 'just touches' the curve at that point (in the sense explained more precisely below.) As it passes through the point of tangency, the _____ is 'going in the same direction' as the curve, and in this sense it is the best straight-line approximation to the curve at that point. The same definition applies to space curves and curves in n-dimensional Euclidean space.

a. Lie derivative
b. North pole
c. Minimal surface
d. Tangent line

6. In vector calculus a conservative vector field is a vector field which is the gradient of a scalar potential. There are two closely related concepts: path independence and _____ vector fields. Every conservative vector field has zero curl (and is thus _____), and every conservative vector field has the path independence property.

a. ACTRAN
b. Irrotational
c. AUSM
d. ALGOR

7. In elementary mathematics, physics, and engineering, a _____ is a geometric object that has both a magnitude (or length), direction and sense, (i.e., orientation along the given direction.) A _____ is frequently represented by a line segment with a definite direction, or graphically as an arrow, connecting an initial point A with a terminal point B, and denoted by

The magnitude of the _____ is the length of the segment and the direction characterizes the displacement of B relative to A: how much one should move the point A to 'carry' it to the point B.

Many algebraic operations on real numbers have close analogues for vectors.

a. 15 theorem
b. Linear partial differential operator
c. Vector
d. BDDC

8. In mathematics a _____ is a construction in vector calculus which associates a vector to every point in a (locally) Euclidean space.

Vector fields are often used in physics to model, for example, the speed and direction of a moving fluid throughout space, or the strength and direction of some force, such as the magnetic or gravitational force, as it changes from point to point.

In the rigorous mathematical treatment, (tangent) vector fields are defined on manifolds as sections of a manifold's tangent bundle.

a. BDDC
b. BIBO stability
c. 15 theorem
d. Vector field

Chapter 2. PRELUDE TO CALCULUS

9. A _____ is perfectly round geometrical object in three-dimensional space, such as the shape of a round ball. Like a circle in two dimensions, a perfect _____ is completely symmetrical around its center, with all points on the surface lying the same distance r from the center point. This distance r is known as the radius of the _____.
   - a. Minimal surface
   - b. North pole
   - c. Tangent line
   - d. Sphere

10. In mathematics, the concept of a '_____' is used to describe the behavior of a function as its argument or input either 'gets close' to some point, or as the argument becomes arbitrarily large; or the behavior of a sequence's elements as their index increases indefinitely. Limits are used in calculus and other branches of mathematical analysis to define derivatives and continuity.

    In formulas, _____ is usually abbreviated as lim

   - a. BIBO stability
   - b. BDDC
   - c. Limit
   - d. 15 theorem

11. In mathematics, _____, first defined by the mathematician Daniel Bernoulli and generalized by Friedrich Bessel, are canonical solutions y(x) of Bessel's differential equation:

$$x^2 \frac{d^2y}{dx^2} + x\frac{dy}{dx} + (x^2 - \alpha^2)y = 0$$

for an arbitrary real or complex number α (the order of the Bessel function.) The most common and important special case is where α is an integer n.

Although α and −α produce the same differential equation, it is conventional to define different _____ for these two orders (e.g., so that the _____ are mostly smooth functions of α.)

   - a. Logarithmic integral function
   - b. Multiplication theorem
   - c. 15 theorem
   - d. Bessel functions

12. The function difference divided by the point difference is known as the _____, it is also known as Newton's quotient):

$$\frac{\Delta F(P)}{\Delta P} = \frac{F(P + \Delta P) - F(P)}{\Delta P} = \frac{\nabla F(P + \Delta P)}{\Delta P}.$$

If ΔP is infinitesimal, then the _____ is a derivative, otherwise it is a divided difference:

$$\text{If } |\Delta P| = \iota ota : \quad \frac{\Delta F(P)}{\Delta P} = \frac{dF(P)}{dP} = F'(P) = G(P);$$

$$\text{If } |\Delta P| > \iota ota : \quad \frac{\Delta F(P)}{\Delta P} = \frac{DF(P)}{DP} = F[P, P + \Delta P].$$

18   *Chapter 2. PRELUDE TO CALCULUS*

Regardless if ΔP is infinitesimal or finite, there is (at least--in the case of the derivative--theoretically) a point range, where the boundaries are $P \pm (.5)\Delta P$ (depending on the orientation--$\Delta F(P)$, $\delta F(P)$ or $\nabla F(P)$):

       LB = Lower Boundary; UB = Upper Boundary;

Anyone familiar with derivatives knows that they can be regarded as functions themselves, harboring their own derivatives. Thus each function is home to sequential degrees ('higher orders') of derivation, or differentiation. This property can be generalized to all difference quotients. As this sequencing requires a corresponding boundary splintering, it is practical to break up the point range into smaller, equi-sized sections, with each section being marked by an intermediary point ('P_i'), where LB = P_0 and UB = P_{A_n}, the nth point, equaling the degree/order:

$LB = P_0 = P_0 + 0\Delta_1 P = P_{A_n} - (Åf\text{-}0)\Delta_1 P$; $P_1 = P_0 + 1\Delta_1 P = P_{A_n} - (Åf\text{-}1)\Delta_1 P$; $P_2 = P_0 + 2\Delta_1 P = P_{A_n} - (Åf\text{-}2)\Delta_1 P$; $P_3 = P_0 + 3\Delta_1 P = P_{A_n} - (Åf\text{-}3)\Delta_1 P$; ↓↓↓↓ $P_{A_n\text{-}3} = P_0 + (Åf\text{-}3)\Delta_1 P = P_{A_n} - 3\Delta_1 P$; $P_{A_n\text{-}2} = P_0 + (Åf\text{-}2)\Delta_1 P = P_{A_n} - 2\Delta_1 P$; $P_{A_n\text{-}1} = P_0 + (Åf\text{-}1)\Delta_1 P = P_{A_n} - 1\Delta_1 P$; $UB = P_{A_n\text{-}0} = P_0 + (Åf\text{-}0)\Delta_1 P = P_{A_n} - 0\Delta_1 P = P_{A_n}$;

$\Delta P = \Delta_1 P = P_1 - P_0 = P_2 - P_1 = P_3 - P_2 = \ldots$

     a. Difference quotient   b. Notation for differentiation
     c. Continuously differentiable   d. Directional derivative

    13.   In calculus, a branch of mathematics, the _____ is a measurement of how a function changes when its input changes. Loosely speaking, a _____ can be thought of as how much a quantity is changing at some given point. For example, the _____ of the position (or distance) of a vehicle with respect to time is the instantaneous velocity (respectively, instantaneous speed) at which the vehicle is traveling.

The process of finding a _____ is called differentiation. The fundamental theorem of calculus states that differentiation is the reverse process to integration.

     a. Semi-differentiability   b. Derivative
     c. Bounded function   d. Stationary phase approximation

    14.   The _____ of any solid, liquid, plasma, vacuum or theoretical object is how much three-dimensional space it occupies, often quantified numerically. One-dimensional figures (such as lines) and two-dimensional shapes (such as squares) are assigned zero _____ in the three-dimensional space. _____ is commonly presented in units such as mL or cm^3 (milliliters or cubic centimeters.)

     a. Dirac equation   b. Vector potential
     c. Klein-Gordon equation   d. Volume

    15.   In the two-dimensional case, a _____ perpendicularly intersects the tangent line to a curve at a given point.

Chapter 2. PRELUDE TO CALCULUS

The _____ is often used in computer graphics to determine a surface's orientation toward a light source for flat shading, or the orientation of each of the corners (vertices) to mimic a curved surface with Phong shading.

For a polygon (such as a triangle), a surface normal can be calculated as the vector cross product of two (non-parallel) edges of the polygon.

- a. Parametric surface
- b. Hyperbolic paraboloid
- c. Normal line
- d. PDE surfaces

16. _____ is how much exposed area an object has. It is expressed in square units. If an object has flat faces, its _____ can be calculated by adding together the areas of its faces.
- a. Vector area
- b. Plane curve
- c. Lipschitz domain
- d. Surface area

17. In mathematics and computer science, the floor and ceiling functions map a real number to the next smallest or next largest integer. More precisely, floor(x) is the largest integer not greater than x and ceiling(x) is the smallest integer not less than x.

The _____ is also called the greatest integer or entier function, and the floor of a nonnegative x may be called the integral part or integral value of x. Computer languages (other than APL) commonly use ENTIER(x) (Algol), floor(x), or int(x) (C and C++).

- a. Hyperbolic functions
- b. Hyperbolic tangent
- c. Floor function
- d. Multiplicative inverse

18. Integration is an important concept in mathematics, specifically in the field of calculus and, more broadly, mathematical analysis. Given a function f of a real variable x and an interval [a, b] of the real line, the _____

$$\int_a^b f(x)\, dx,$$

is defined informally to be the net signed area of the region in the xy-plane bounded by the graph of f, the x-axis, and the vertical lines x = a and x = b.

The term '_____' may also refer to the notion of antiderivative, a function F whose derivative is the given function f.

- a. Indefinite integral
- b. Integrand
- c. Integral test for convergence
- d. Integral

19. The _____ is the equation of state of a hypothetical ideal gas, first stated by Benoît Paul Émile Clapeyron in 1834. The law is derived from the fact that in the ideal state of any gas a given number of its 'particles' occupy the same volume, and that volume changes are inverse to pressure changes and linear to temperature changes.

The state of an amount of gas is determined by its pressure, volume, and temperature according to the equation:

$$pV = nRT$$

where

> p is the absolute pressure of the gas,
> V is the volume of the gas,
> n is the number of moles of gas,
> R is the universal gas constant,
> T is the absolute temperature.

a. Ideal gas law
c. AUSM
b. ACTRAN
d. ALGOR

20. Any formula written in terms of logarithms may be said to be in _____.

In contexts including complex manifolds and algebraic geometry, a logarithmic differential form is a 1-form that, locally at least, can be written

$$\frac{df}{f}$$

for some meromorphic function (resp. rational function) f.

a. Holomorphic sheaf
c. LOGARITHMIC FORM
b. Bifurcation locus
d. Cayley transform

21. _____ is the word created by Gilles de Roberval for the curve described by a fixed point as a circle rolls along a straight line. As a circle of radius a rolls without slipping along a line L, the center C moves parallel to L, and every other point P in the rotating plane rigidly attached to the circle traces the curve called the _____. Let CP = b. If P lies inside the circle (b < a), on its circumference (b = a), or outside (b > a), the _____ is described as being curtate, common, or prolate, respectively.

a. Trochoid
c. Witch of Agnesi
b. Hypocycloid
d. Kappa curve

22. In mathematics, the _____ is an extension of the factorial function to real and complex numbers. For a complex number z with positive real part the _____ is defined by

$$\Gamma(z) = \int_0^\infty t^{z-1} e^{-t}\, dt\ .$$

This definition can be extended to the rest of the complex plane, excepting the non-positive integers.

If n is a positive integer, then

$\Gamma(n) = (n - 1)!$,

showing the connection to the factorial function.

a. Digamma function
c. Pochhammer k-symbol
b. Multivariate gamma function
d. Gamma function

23. In elementary algebra, a _____ is a polynomial with two terms--the sum of two monomials--often bound by parenthesis or brackets when operated upon. It is the simplest kind of polynomial other than monomials.

- The _____ $a^2 - b^2$ can be factored as the product of two other binomials:

    $a^2 - b^2 = (a + b)(a - b.)$

    This is a special case of the more general formula:

    $$a^{n+1} - b^{n+1} = (a - b) \sum_{k=0}^{n} a^k b^{n-k}$$

- The product of a pair of linear binomials $(ax + b)$ and $(cx + d)$ is:

    $(ax + b)(cx + d) = acx^2 + axd + bcx + bd$.

- A _____ raised to the nth power, represented as

    $(a + b)^n$

    can be expanded by means of the _____ theorem or, equivalently, using Pascal's triangle. Taking a simple example, the perfect square _____ $(p + q)^2$ can be found by squaring the first digit, adding twice the product of the first and second digit and finally adding the square of the second digit, to give $p^2 + 2pq + q^2$.

a. Binomial
c. Completing the square
b. Multinomial theorem
d. Partial fractions

24. In mathematics, the _____ generalizes the purely algebraic formula of the binomial theorem to complex values of α. It is also a special case of a Newton series. The _____ is the series

$$(1 + x)^\alpha = \sum_{k=0}^{\infty} \binom{\alpha}{k} x^k = \sum_{k=0}^{\infty} \frac{\prod_{a=0}^{k-1}(\alpha - a)\, x^k}{k!}$$

where α is a complex number and

$$\binom{\alpha}{k} = \frac{\alpha(\alpha - 1)(\alpha - 2) \cdots (\alpha - k + 1)}{k!}$$

is the (generalized) binomial coefficient (if α is a non negative integer, then the (α + 1) th term and all later terms in the series are zero, since each one contains a factor equal to (α − α): thus, in that case, the summation reduces to the algebraic binomial formula.)

a. Maxima
b. Differential
c. Fresnel integrals
d. Binomial series

25. If a particular point on a sphere is (arbitrarily) designated as its _____, then the corresponding antipodal point is called the south pole and the equator is the great circle that is equidistant to them. Great circles through the two poles are called lines (or meridians) of longitude, and the line connecting the two poles is called the axis of rotation. Circles on the sphere that are parallel to the equator are lines of latitude.

a. Minimal surface
b. Tangent line
c. North pole
d. Sphere

26. The _____, formerly known as the hyperbolic logarithm, is the logarithm to the base e, where e is an irrational constant approximately equal to 2.718281828. It is also sometimes referred to as the Napierian logarithm, although the original meaning of this term is slightly different. In simple terms, the _____ of a number x is the power to which e would have to be raised to equal x -- for example the natural log of e itself is 1 because e^1 = e, while the _____ of 1 would be 0, since e^0 = 1.

a. BIBO stability
b. BDDC
c. 15 theorem
d. Natural logarithm

27. Trigonometry is a branch of mathematics that deals with triangles, particularly those plane triangles in which one angle has 90 degrees (right triangles.) Trigonometry deals with relationships between the sides and the angles of triangles and with the _____ functions, which describe those relationships.

Trigonometry has applications in both pure mathematics and in applied mathematics, where it is essential in many branches of science and technology.

a. Trigonometric functions
b. Sine
c. Trigonometric
d. Trigonometric integrals

28. In calculus, a _____ is either of the two limits of a function f(x) of a real variable x as x approaches a specified point either from below or from above. One should write either:

$$\lim_{x \to a^+} f(x) \text{ or } \lim_{x \downarrow a} f(x)$$

for the limit as x decreases in value approaching a (x approaches a 'from above' or 'from the right'), and similarly

$$\lim_{x \to a^-} f(x) \text{ or } \lim_{x \uparrow a} f(x)$$

for the limit as x increases in value approaching a (x approaches a 'from below' or 'from the left'.)

Chapter 2. PRELUDE TO CALCULUS

The two one-sided limits exist and are equal if and only if the limit of f(x) as x approaches a exists.

a. AUSM
b. ALGOR
c. ACTRAN
d. One-sided limit

29. In a totally ordered set all elements are mutually comparable, so such a set can have at most one minimal element and at most one maximal element. Then, due to mutual comparability, the minimal element will also be the least element and the maximal element will also be the greatest element. Thus in a totally ordered set we can simply use the terms minimum and _____.

a. Racetrack principle
b. Maximum
c. Leibniz rule
d. Nth term

30. In a totally ordered set all elements are mutually comparable, so such a set can have at most one minimal element and at most one maximal element. Then, due to mutual comparability, the minimal element will also be the least element and the maximal element will also be the greatest element. Thus in a totally ordered set we can simply use the terms _____ and maximum.

a. Minimum
b. Ghosts of departed quantities
c. Maximum
d. Nth term

31. Cantor defined two kinds of _____ numbers, the ordinal numbers and the cardinal numbers. Ordinal numbers may be identified with well-ordered sets, or counting carried on to any stopping point, including points after an _____ number have already been counted. Generalizing finite and the ordinary _____ sequences which are maps from the positive integers leads to mappings from ordinal numbers, and transfinite sequences.

a. ALGOR
b. Infinite
c. ACTRAN
d. AUSM

32. Continuous functions are of utmost importance in mathematics and applications. However, not all functions are continuous. If a function is not continuous at a point in its domain, one says that it has a _____ there. The set of all points of _____ of a function may be a discrete set, a dense set, or even the entire domain of the function.

a. Vector
b. 15 theorem
c. BDDC
d. Discontinuity

33. In mathematics, _____ refers to any of a number of loosely related concepts in different areas of geometry. Intuitively, _____ is the amount by which a geometric object deviates from being flat, or straight in the case of a line, but this is defined in different ways depending on the context. There is a key distinction between extrinsic _____, which is defined for objects embedded in another space (usually a Euclidean space) in a way that relates to the radius of _____ of circles that touch the object, and intrinsic _____, which is defined at each point in a differential manifold.

a. Minimal surface
b. Lie derivative
c. Curvature
d. Sphere

34. In mathematics, a (topological) _____ is defined as follows: let I be an interval of real numbers (i.e. a non-empty connected subset of $\mathbb{R}$); then a _____ γ is a continuous mapping $\gamma : I \to X$, where X is a topological space. The _____ γ is said to be simple if it is injective, i.e. if for all x, y in I, we have $\gamma(x) = \gamma(y) \implies x = y$. If I is a closed bounded interval $[a, b]$, we also allow the possibility $\gamma(a) = \gamma(b)$ (this convention makes it possible to talk about closed simple _____.)

  a. Closed curve
  b. Prolate cycloid
  c. Tractrix
  d. Curve

35. In infinitesimal calculus, a _____ is traditionally an infinitesimally small change in a variable. For example, if x is a variable, then a change in the value of x is often denoted Δx (or δx when this change is considered to be small.) The _____ dx represents such a change, but is infinitely small.

  a. The Method of Mechanical Theorems
  b. Local maximum
  c. Dirichlet integral
  d. Differential

36. The _____ of a biological species in an environment is the population size of the species that the environment can sustain in the long term, given the food, habitat, water and other necessities available in the environment. For the human population, more complex variables such as sanitation and medical care are sometimes considered as part of the necessary infrastructure.

As population density increases, birth rate often increases and death rate typically decreases.

  a. 15 theorem
  b. Carrying capacity
  c. BIBO stability
  d. BDDC

37. In mathematics, the _____ is used to determine each point uniquely in a plane through two numbers, usually called the x-coordinate or abscissa and the y-coordinate or ordinate of the point. To define the coordinates, two perpendicular directed lines, are specified, as well as the unit length, which is marked off on the two axes Cartesian coordinate systems are also used in space and in higher dimensions.

  a. 15 theorem
  b. Coordinate
  c. Cartesian coordinate system
  d. Cylindrical coordinate system

38. In mathematics, a _____ is any function which can be written as the ratio of two polynomial functions.

$$y = \frac{x^2 - 3x - 2}{x^2 - 4}$$

In the case of one variable, x, a _____ is a function of the form

$$f(x) = \frac{P(x)}{Q(x)}$$

where P and Q are polynomial function in x and Q is not the zero polynomial. The domain of f is the set of all points x for which the denominator Q(x) is not zero.

Chapter 2. PRELUDE TO CALCULUS

a. Rational function
b. 15 theorem
c. BIBO stability
d. BDDC

39. In mathematics, the _____ are functions of an angle. They are important in the study of triangles and modeling periodic phenomena, among many other applications. _____ are commonly defined as ratios of two sides of a right triangle containing the angle, and can equivalently be defined as the lengths of various line segments from a unit circle.
a. Sine integral
b. Trigonometric integrals
c. Trigonometric
d. Trigonometric functions

40. In physics and geometry, the _____ is the theoretical shape of a hanging flexible chain or cable when supported at its ends and acted upon by a uniform gravitational force (its own weight) and in equilibrium. The curve has a U shape that is similar in appearance to the parabola, though it is a different curve.
a. BDDC
b. Catenary
c. 15 theorem
d. BIBO stability

41. _____ is any physical or virtual entity that is owned by an individual or jointly by a group of individuals. An owner of _____ has the right to consume, sell, rent, mortgage, transfer and exchange his or her _____. Important widely-recognized types of _____ include real _____, personal _____ (other physical possessions), and intellectual _____ (rights over artistic creations, inventions, etc.), although the latter is not always as widely recognized or enforced.
a. Property
b. 15 theorem
c. BIBO stability
d. BDDC

42. In computer science and information science, _____ could also be a method or an algorithm. Again, an example will illustrate: There are systems of counting, as with Roman numerals, and various systems for filing papers, or catalogues, and various library systems, of which the Dewey Decimal _____ is an example. This still fits with the definition of components which are connected together (in this case in order to facilitate the flow of information.)
a. BIBO stability
b. 15 theorem
c. System
d. BDDC

Chapter 3. THE DERIVATIVE

1. _____ typically refers to a state lacking order or predictability. In ancient Greece, it referred to the initial state of the universe, and, by extension, space, darkness, or an abyss. In modern English, it is used in classical studies with this original meaning; in mathematics and science to refer to a very specific kind of unpredictability; and informally to mean a state of confusion.
   - a. Chaos
   - b. BIBO stability
   - c. BDDC
   - d. 15 theorem

2. _____ is usually defined as the activity of using and developing computer technology, computer hardware and software. It is the computer-specific part of information technology. Computer science (or _____ science) is the study and the science of the theoretical foundations of information and computation and their implementation and application in computer systems.
   - a. 15 theorem
   - b. BDDC
   - c. Computing
   - d. BIBO stability

3. In infinitesimal calculus, a _____ is traditionally an infinitesimally small change in a variable. For example, if x is a variable, then a change in the value of x is often denoted Δx (or δx when this change is considered to be small.) The _____ dx represents such a change, but is infinitely small.
   - a. Dirichlet integral
   - b. Local maximum
   - c. The Method of Mechanical Theorems
   - d. Differential

4. A _____ is a mathematical equation for an unknown function of one or several variables that relates the values of the function itself and of its derivatives of various orders. they play a prominent role in engineering, physics, economics and other disciplines.

   A simplified real world example of a _____ is modeling the acceleration of a ball falling through the air (considering only gravity and air resistance.)

   - a. Phase line
   - b. Caloric polynomial
   - c. Structural stability
   - d. Differential Equation

5. In calculus, a branch of mathematics, the _____ is a measurement of how a function changes when its input changes. Loosely speaking, a _____ can be thought of as how much a quantity is changing at some given point. For example, the _____ of the position (or distance) of a vehicle with respect to time is the instantaneous velocity (respectively, instantaneous speed) at which the vehicle is traveling.

   The process of finding a _____ is called differentiation. The fundamental theorem of calculus states that differentiation is the reverse process to integration.

   - a. Semi-differentiability
   - b. Stationary phase approximation
   - c. Derivative
   - d. Bounded function

6. _____ is used to describe the steepness, incline, gradient, or grade of a straight line. A higher _____ value indicates a steeper incline. The _____ is defined as the ratio of the 'rise' divided by the 'run' between two points on a line, or in other words, the ratio of the altitude change to the horizontal distance between any two points on the line.
   - a. Y-intercept
   - b. Sequence
   - c. 15 theorem
   - d. Slope

Chapter 3. THE DERIVATIVE

7. A _____, in mathematics, is a polynomial function of the form $f(x) = ax^2 + bx + c$, where $a \neq 0$. The graph of a _____ is a parabola whose major axis is parallel to the y-axis.

The expression ax² + bx + c in the definition of a _____ is a polynomial of degree 2 or a 2nd degree polynomial, because the highest exponent of x is 2.

    a. Leading coefficient   b. Resultant
    c. Discriminant   d. Quadratic function

8. In elementary mathematics, physics, and engineering, a _____ is a geometric object that has both a magnitude (or length), direction and sense, (i.e., orientation along the given direction.) A _____ is frequently represented by a line segment with a definite direction, or graphically as an arrow, connecting an initial point A with a terminal point B, and denoted by

The magnitude of the _____ is the length of the segment and the direction characterizes the displacement of B relative to A: how much one should move the point A to 'carry' it to the point B.

Many algebraic operations on real numbers have close analogues for vectors.

    a. BDDC   b. Linear partial differential operator
    c. Vector   d. 15 theorem

9. In physics, _____ is defined as the rate of change of position. it is vector physical quantity; both speed and direction are required to define it. In the SI (metric) system, it is measured in meters per second: (m/s) or ms⁻¹.
    a. 15 theorem   b. BDDC
    c. Velocity   d. BIBO stability

10. In physics, and more specifically kinematics, _____ is the change in velocity over time. Because velocity is a vector, it can change in two ways: a change in magnitude and/or a change in direction. In one dimension, _____ is the rate at which something speeds up or slows down.
    a. Acceleration   b. AUSM
    c. ACTRAN   d. ALGOR

11. Integration is an important concept in mathematics, specifically in the field of calculus and, more broadly, mathematical analysis. Given a function f of a real variable x and an interval [a, b] of the real line, the _____

$$\int_a^b f(x)\,dx,$$

is defined informally to be the net signed area of the region in the xy-plane bounded by the graph of f, the x-axis, and the vertical lines x = a and x = b.

Chapter 3. THE DERIVATIVE

The term '_____' may also refer to the notion of antiderivative, a function F whose derivative is the given function f.

a. Integrand
b. Integral
c. Indefinite integral
d. Integral test for convergence

12. This article will state and prove the _____ for differentiation, and then use it to prove these two formulas.

The _____ for differentiation states that for every natural number n, the derivative of $f(x) = x^n$ is $f'(x) = nx^{n-1}$, that is,

$$(x^n)' = nx^{n-1}.$$

The _____ for integration

$$\int x^n \, dx = \frac{x^{n+1}}{n+1} + C$$

for natural n is then an easy consequence. One just needs to take the derivative of this equality and use the _____ and linearity of differentiation on the right-hand side.

a. Power rule
b. Leibniz rule
c. Test for Divergence
d. Functional integration

13. A _____ is the location at which two or more bones make contact. They are constructed to allow movement and provide mechanical support, and are classified structurally and functionally. Depiction of an intervertebral disk, a cartilaginous _____. Diagram of a synovial (diarthrosis) _____.

Joints are mainly classified structurally and functionally.

a. BDDC
b. Joint
c. 15 theorem
d. BIBO stability

14. In mathematics, _____ are a concept central to linear algebra and related fields of mathematics

Suppose that K is a field and V is a vector space over K. As usual, we call elements of V vectors and call elements of K scalars.

a. 15 theorem
b. Linear combinations
c. Fundamental theorem of algebra
d. Permutation

15. In calculus, the _____ is a method of finding the derivative of a function that is the quotient of two other functions for which derivatives exist.

If the function one wishes to differentiate, f(x), can be written as

$$f(x) = \frac{g(x)}{h(x)}$$

and h(x) ≠ 0, then the rule states that the derivative of g(x) / h(x) is equal to:

$$\frac{d}{dx}f(x) = f'(x) = \frac{g'(x)h(x) - g(x)h'(x)}{[h(x)]^2}.$$

Or, more precisely, if all x in some open set containing the number a satisfy h(x) ≠ 0; and g'(a) and h'(a) both exist; then, f'(a) exists as well and:

$$f'(a) = \frac{g'(a)h(a) - g(a)h'(a)}{[h(a)]^2}.$$

The derivative of (4x − 2) / (x² + 1) is:

$$\frac{d}{dx}\left[\frac{(4x-2)}{x^2+1}\right] = \frac{(x^2+1)(4) - (4x-2)(2x)}{(x^2+1)^2}$$
$$= \frac{(4x^2+4) - (8x^2-4x)}{(x^2+1)^2} = \frac{-4x^2+4x+4}{(x^2+1)^2}$$

In the example above, the choices

g(x) = 4x − 2
h(x) = x² + 1

were made. Analogously, the derivative of sin(x) / x² (when x ≠ 0) is:

$$\frac{\cos(x)x^2 - \sin(x)2x}{x^4}$$

Another example is:

$$f(x) = \frac{2x^2}{x^3}$$

whereas g(x) = 2x² and h(x) = x³, and g'(x) = 4x and h'(x) = 3x².

    a. Quotient rule
    b. Differentiation rules
    c. Constant factor rule in differentiation
    d. Reciprocal Rule

16. The _____ of any solid, liquid, plasma, vacuum or theoretical object is how much three-dimensional space it occupies, often quantified numerically. One-dimensional figures (such as lines) and two-dimensional shapes (such as squares) are assigned zero _____ in the three-dimensional space. _____ is commonly presented in units such as mL or cm³ (milliliters or cubic centimeters.)

    a. Dirac equation
    b. Klein-Gordon equation
    c. Vector potential
    d. Volume

17. In calculus, the _____ is a formula used to find the derivatives of products of functions. It may be stated thus:

$$(f \cdot g)' = f' \cdot g + f \cdot g'$$

or in the Leibniz notation thus:

$$\frac{d}{dx}(u \cdot v) = u \cdot \frac{dv}{dx} + v \cdot \frac{du}{dx}.$$

Discovery of this rule is credited to Gottfried Leibniz, who demonstrated it using differentials. Here is Leibniz's argument: Let u and v be two differentiable functions of x.

    a. Quotient Rule
    b. Constant factor rule in differentiation
    c. Differentiation rules
    d. Product rule

18. In calculus, the _____ is a shorthand method of finding the derivative of a function that is the reciprocal of a differentiable function, without using the quotient rule or chain rule.

The _____ states that the derivative of 1 / g(x) is given by

$$\frac{d}{dx}\left(\frac{1}{g(x)}\right) = \frac{-g'(x)}{(g(x))^2}$$

where $g(x) \neq 0$.

The _____ is derived from the quotient rule, with the numerator f(x) = 1. Then,

It is also possible to derive the _____ from the chain rule, by a process very much like that of the derivation of the quotient rule.

- a. Product rule
- b. Differentiation rules
- c. Quotient Rule
- d. Reciprocal rule

19. In a totally ordered set all elements are mutually comparable, so such a set can have at most one minimal element and at most one maximal element. Then, due to mutual comparability, the minimal element will also be the least element and the maximal element will also be the greatest element. Thus in a totally ordered set we can simply use the terms minimum and _____.

- a. Leibniz rule
- b. Racetrack principle
- c. Nth term
- d. Maximum

20. In calculus, the _____ is a formula for the derivative of the composite of two functions.

In intuitive terms, if a variable, y, depends on a second variable, u, which in turn depends on a third variable, x, then the rate of change of y with respect to x can be computed as the rate of change of y with respect to u multiplied by the rate of change of u with respect to x. Schematically,

$$\frac{dy}{dx} = \frac{dy}{du} \cdot \frac{du}{dx}.$$

- a. Chain rule
- b. Product rule
- c. Reciprocal Rule
- d. Differentiation rules

21. In probability theory and statistics, the _____ (or expectation value or mean and for continuous random variables with a density function it is the probability density -weighted integral of the possible values.

The term '_____' can be misleading.

- a. ALGOR
- b. ACTRAN
- c. AUSM
- d. Expected value

22. In calculus, the _____ states, roughly, that given a section of a smooth curve, there is at least one point on that section at which the derivative (slope) of the curve is equal (parallel) to the 'average' derivative of the section. It is used to prove theorems that make global conclusions about a function on an interval starting from local hypotheses about derivatives at points of the interval.

This theorem can be understood concretely by applying it to motion: If a car travels one hundred miles in one hour, so its average speed during that time was 100 miles per hour.

a. Periodic function
b. Limits of integration
c. Hyperbolic angle
d. Mean value theorem

23. In mathematics, the _____ (or modulus) of a real number is its numerical value without regard to its sign. So, for example, 3 is the _____ of both 3 and −3.

The _____ of a number a is denoted by $|\,a\,|$.

a. Area hyperbolic functions
b. ACTRAN
c. Absolute value
d. Exponential function

24. In geometry, the _____ (or simply the tangent) to a curve at a given point is the straight line that 'just touches' the curve at that point (in the sense explained more precisely below.) As it passes through the point of tangency, the _____ is 'going in the same direction' as the curve, and in this sense it is the best straight-line approximation to the curve at that point. The same definition applies to space curves and curves in n-dimensional Euclidean space.

a. North pole
b. Tangent line
c. Lie derivative
d. Minimal surface

25. f'(x) is twice the absolute value function, and it does not have a derivative at zero. Similar examples show that a function can have k derivatives for any non-negative integer k but no (k + 1)-order derivative. A function that has k successive derivatives is called _____.

a. Power series
b. Differential calculus
c. Differential coefficient
d. K times differentiable

26. In a totally ordered set all elements are mutually comparable, so such a set can have at most one minimal element and at most one maximal element. Then, due to mutual comparability, the minimal element will also be the least element and the maximal element will also be the greatest element. Thus in a totally ordered set we can simply use the terms _____ and maximum.

a. Nth term
b. Ghosts of departed quantities
c. Maximum
d. Minimum

27. A real-valued function f defined on the real line is said to have a _____ point at the point $x^{>*}$, if there exists some $>\varepsilon > 0$, such that $f(x^{>*}) \geq f(x)$ when $|x >- x^{>*}| < >\varepsilon$. The value of the function at this point is called maximum of the function.

On a graph of a function, its local maxima will look like the tops of hills.

a. Test for Divergence
b. Racetrack principle
c. Standard part function
d. Local Maximum

28. In mathematics, a _____ (or critical number) is a point on the domain of a function where:

- one dimension: the derivative (or slope of the line when visualized) is equal to zero or a point where the function ceases to be differentiable.
- in general: there are two distinct concepts: either the derivative (Jacobian) vanishes, or it is not of full rank (or, in either case, the function is not differentiable); these agree in one dimension.

Note that in one dimension, a critical value or critical number x of function f is the domain element at which the derivative is zero or undefined, whereas the associated ordered pair (x, y) is the _____. In higher dimensions a critical value is in the range whereas a _____ is in the domain.

There are two situations in which a point becomes a _____ of a function of one variable. The first of which is that the value of the first derivative is equal to zero.

- a. Differentiation operator
- b. Multivariable calculus
- c. Total derivative
- d. Critical point

29. In mathematics and computer science, the floor and ceiling functions map a real number to the next smallest or next largest integer. More precisely, floor(x) is the largest integer not greater than x and ceiling(x) is the smallest integer not less than x.

The _____ is also called the greatest integer or entier function, and the floor of a nonnegative x may be called the integral part or integral value of x. Computer languages (other than APL) commonly use ENTIER(x) (Algol), floor(x), or int(x) (C and C++).

- a. Hyperbolic tangent
- b. Multiplicative inverse
- c. Hyperbolic functions
- d. Floor function

30. In geometry, the _____, geometric center, or barycenter of a plane figure X is the intersection of all straight lines that divide X into two parts of equal moment about the line. Informally, it is the 'average' of all points of X. The definition extends to any object X in n-dimensional space: its _____ is the intersection of all hyperplanes that divide X into two parts of equal moment.

- a. BIBO stability
- b. 15 theorem
- c. BDDC
- d. Centroid

31. In optics, _____ or the principle of least time is the idea that the path taken between two points by a ray of light is the path that can be traversed in the least time. This principle is sometimes taken as the definition of a ray of light.

_____ can be used to describe the properties of light rays reflected off mirrors, refracted through different media, or undergoing total internal reflection. It can be deduced from Huygens' principle, and can be used to derive Snell's law of refraction and the law of reflection.

- a. Fermat's Principle
- b. BIBO stability
- c. 15 theorem
- d. BDDC

32. The _____ of an angle is the ratio of the length of the adjacent side to the length of the hypotenuse. In our case

$$\cos A = \frac{\text{adjacent}}{\text{hypotenuse}} = \frac{b}{h}.$$

The tangent of an angle is the ratio of the length of the opposite side to the length of the adjacent side. In our case

$$\tan A = \frac{\text{opposite}}{\text{adjacent}} = \frac{a}{b}.$$

The remaining three functions are best defined using the above three functions.

    a. Trigonometric   b. Trigonometric functions
    c. Sine integral   d. Cosine

33. The _____ of an angle is the ratio of the length of the opposite side to the length of the hypotenuse. In our case

$$\sin A = \frac{\text{opposite}}{\text{hypotenuse}} = \frac{a}{h}.$$

Note that this ratio does not depend on size of the particular right triangle chosen, as long as it contains the angle A, since all such triangles are similar.

The cosine of an angle is the ratio of the length of the adjacent side to the length of the hypotenuse.

    a. Trigonometric functions   b. Trigonometric
    c. Sine integral   d. Sine

34. Trigonometry is a branch of mathematics that deals with triangles, particularly those plane triangles in which one angle has 90 degrees (right triangles.) Trigonometry deals with relationships between the sides and the angles of triangles and with the _____ functions, which describe those relationships.

Trigonometry has applications in both pure mathematics and in applied mathematics, where it is essential in many branches of science and technology.

    a. Trigonometric integrals   b. Trigonometric functions
    c. Trigonometric   d. Sine

35. In mathematics, the _____ are functions of an angle. They are important in the study of triangles and modeling periodic phenomena, among many other applications. _____ are commonly defined as ratios of two sides of a right triangle containing the angle, and can equivalently be defined as the lengths of various line segments from a unit circle.
    a. Sine integral   b. Trigonometric integrals
    c. Trigonometric   d. Trigonometric functions

36. In mathematics, the _____ are analogs of the ordinary trigonometric or circular functions. The basic _____ are the hyperbolic sine 'sinh', and the hyperbolic cosine 'cosh', from which are derived the hyperbolic tangent 'tanh', etc., in analogy to the derived trigonometric functions. The inverse _____ are the area hyperbolic sine 'arsinh' (also called 'asinh', or sometimes by the misnomer of 'arcsinh') and so on.

Chapter 3. THE DERIVATIVE

a. Signum function
c. Multiplicative inverse
b. Hyperbolic cosine
d. Hyperbolic functions

37. The _____ is a function in mathematics. The application of this function to a value x is written as exp(x). Equivalently, this can be written in the form e^x, where e is a mathematical constant, the base of the natural logarithm, which equals approximately 2.718281828, and is also known as Euler's number.
   a. Area hyperbolic functions
   c. ACTRAN
   b. Integral part
   d. Exponential function

38. In mathematics, a _____ differential equation may refer to one of two related things, both of which are differential equations that can be attacked by a method of separation of variables.

   - For ordinary differential equations, it describes a class of equations that can be separated into a pair of integrals. See: Examples of differential equations

   - For partial differential equations, it describes a class of equations that can be broken down into differential equations in fewer independent variables. See _____ partial differential equation.

   a. Method of undetermined coefficients
   c. Lax pair
   b. Differential equation
   d. Separable

39. An _____ is a type of quadric surface that is a higher dimensional analogue of an ellipse. The equation of a standard axis-aligned _____ body in an xyz-Cartesian coordinate system is

$$\frac{x^2}{a^2} + \frac{y^2}{b^2} + \frac{z^2}{c^2} = 1$$

where a and b are the equatorial radii (along the x and y axes) and c is the polar radius (along the z-axis), all of which are fixed positive real numbers determining the shape of the _____.

More generally, a not-necessarily-axis-aligned _____ is defined by the equation

$$\mathbf{x}^T A \mathbf{x} = 1$$

where A is a symmetric positive definite matrix and x is a vector.

   a. ALGOR
   c. Ellipsoid
   b. AUSM
   d. ACTRAN

40. The function $\log_b(x)$ depends on both b and x, but the term _____ in standard usage refers to a function of the form $\log_b(x)$ in which the base b is fixed and so the only argument is x. Thus there is one _____ for each value of the base b (which must be positive and must differ from 1.) Viewed in this way, the base-b _____ is the inverse function of the exponential function b^x.

a. BDDC
b. BIBO stability
c. 15 theorem
d. Logarithm function

41. In mathematics, the _____ of a function y = f(x) is a function that, in some fashion, 'undoes' the effect of f The _____ of f is denoted f^{-1}. The statements y=f(x) and x=f^{-1}(y) are equivalent.
   a. AUSM
   b. ALGOR
   c. Inverse
   d. ACTRAN

42. In mathematics, if f is a function from A to B then an _____ for f is a function in the opposite direction, from B to A, with the property that a round trip (a composition) from A to B to A (or from B to A to B) returns each element of the initial set to itself. Thus, if an input x into the function f produces an output y, then inputting y into the _____ f^{-1} (read f inverse, not to be confused with exponentiation) produces the output x. Not every function has an inverse; those that do are called invertible.
   a. Augustin Louis Cauchy
   b. Aristotle
   c. Augustin-Jean Fresnel
   d. Inverse function

43. In mathematics, an _____, is the apparent shape of a circle viewed obliquely from outside it, as distinct from a hyperbola which is the shape seen from inside. It is the finite or bounded case of a conic section as a shape cut in a cone by a plane, the unbounded cases being the parabola, which like the _____ remains connected, and the hyperbola, which separates into two connected components or branches.

Equivalently an _____ can be defined as the locus of points, or path traced out, in a plane such that the sum of the distances from the moving point to two fixed points remains constant.

   a. ALGOR
   b. AUSM
   c. ACTRAN
   d. Ellipse

44. In mathematics, the _____ is a conic section, the intersection of a right circular conical surface and a plane parallel to a generating straight line of that surface. Given a point (the focus) and a line (the directrix) that lie in a plane, the locus of points in that plane that are equidistant to them is a _____.

A particular case arises when the plane is tangent to the conical surface of a circle.

   a. BDDC
   b. BIBO stability
   c. 15 theorem
   d. Parabola

45. The _____, formerly known as the hyperbolic logarithm, is the logarithm to the base e, where e is an irrational constant approximately equal to 2.718281828. It is also sometimes referred to as the Napierian logarithm, although the original meaning of this term is slightly different. In simple terms, the _____ of a number x is the power to which e would have to be raised to equal x -- for example the natural log of e itself is 1 because e^1 = e, while the _____ of 1 would be 0, since e^0 = 1.
   a. BIBO stability
   b. 15 theorem
   c. BDDC
   d. Natural logarithm

46. In mathematics, specifically in calculus and complex analysis, the _____ of a function f is defined by the formula

$$\frac{f'}{f}$$

where f ' is the derivative of f.

When f is a function f(x) of a real variable x, and takes real, strictly positive values, this is indeed the formula for (log f)', that is, the derivative of the natural logarithm of f, as follows directly from the chain rule.

Many properties of the real logarithm also apply to the _____, even when the function does not take values in the positive reals.

    a. Point of inflection   b. Lin-Tsien equation
    c. Logarithmic derivative   d. Directional derivative

47.   In calculus, a method called _____ can be applied to implicitly defined functions. This method is an application of the chain rule allowing one to calculate the derivative of a function given implicitly.

As explained in the introduction, y can be given as a function of x implicitly rather than explicitly. When we have an equation R (x,y) = 0, we may be able to solve it for y and then differentiate. However, sometimes it is simpler to differentiate R(x,y) with respect to x and then solve for dy / dx.

    a. Implicit function   b. Implicit differentiation
    c. Ordinary differential equation   d. Automatic differentiation

48.   In Geometry, the _____ is an algebraic curve defined by the equation

$$x^3 + y^3 - 3axy = 0$$

It forms a loop in the first quadrant with a double point at the origin and asymptote

$$x + y + a = 0$$

It is symmetrical about y = x.

    a. Curve   b. Folium of Descartes
    c. Cochleoid   d. Prolate cycloid

49.   In mathematics, a _____ is an ordered list of objects (or events). Like a set, it contains members (also called elements or terms), and the number of terms (possibly infinite) is called the length of the _____. Unlike a set, order matters, and the exact same elements can appear multiple times at different positions in the _____.
    a. Slope   b. Y-intercept
    c. 15 theorem   d. Sequence

50. In mathematics, _____, first defined by the mathematician Daniel Bernoulli and generalized by Friedrich Bessel, are canonical solutions y(x) of Bessel's differential equation:

$$x^2 \frac{d^2y}{dx^2} + x\frac{dy}{dx} + (x^2 - \alpha^2)y = 0$$

for an arbitrary real or complex number α (the order of the Bessel function.) The most common and important special case is where α is an integer n.

Although α and −α produce the same differential equation, it is conventional to define different _____ for these two orders (e.g., so that the _____ are mostly smooth functions of α.)

- a. Logarithmic integral function
- b. Multiplication theorem
- c. Bessel functions
- d. 15 theorem

51. In mathematics, the complex numbers are an extension of the real numbers obtained by adjoining an imaginary unit, denoted i.

Every _____ can be written in the form a + bi, where a and b are real numbers called the real part and the imaginary part of the _____, respectively.

Complex numbers are a field, and thus have addition, subtraction, multiplication, and division operations. These operations extend the corresponding operations on real numbers, although with a number of additional elegant and useful properties, e.g., negative real numbers can be obtained by squaring complex (imaginary) numbers.

- a. Complex number
- b. Filled Julia set
- c. Real part
- d. Conjugated line

52. _____ is the long dimension of any object. The _____ of a thing is the distance between its ends, its linear extent as measured from end to end. This may be distinguished from height, which is vertical extent, and width or breadth, which are the distance from side to side, measuring across the object at right angles to the _____.
- a. 15 theorem
- b. BIBO stability
- c. BDDC
- d. Length

53. If a particular point on a sphere is (arbitrarily) designated as its _____, then the corresponding antipodal point is called the south pole and the equator is the great circle that is equidistant to them. Great circles through the two poles are called lines (or meridians) of longitude, and the line connecting the two poles is called the axis of rotation. Circles on the sphere that are parallel to the equator are lines of latitude.
- a. Tangent line
- b. Minimal surface
- c. Sphere
- d. North pole

Chapter 4. ADDITIONAL APPLICATIONS OF THE DERIVATIVE

1. In mathematics, a _____ is an approximation of a general function using a linear function (more precisely, an affine function.)

Given a differentiable function f of one real variable, Taylor's theorem for n=1 states that

$$f(x) = f(a) + f\,'(a)(x-a) + R_2$$

where R_2 is the remainder term. The _____ is obtained by dropping the remainder:

$$f(x) \approx f(a) + f\,'(a)(x-a)$$

which is true for x close to a.

- a. Point of inflection
- b. Lin-Tsien equation
- c. Smooth function
- d. Linear approximation

2. In algebra, a _____ is a function depending on n that associates a scalar, det(A), to an n×n square matrix A. The fundamental geometric meaning of a _____ is a scale factor for measure when A is regarded as a linear transformation. Determinants are important both in calculus, where they enter the substitution rule for several variables, and in multilinear algebra.

For a fixed nonnegative integer n, there is a unique _____ function for the n×n matrices over any commutative ring R. In particular, this function exists when R is the field of real or complex numbers.

- a. BIBO stability
- b. Determinant
- c. 15 theorem
- d. BDDC

3. The _____ in some data is the discrepancy between an exact value and some approximation to it. An _____ can occur because

   1. the measurement of the data is not precise (due to the instruments), or
   2. approximations are used instead of the real data (e.g., 3.14 instead of π.)

In the mathematical field of numerical analysis, the numerical stability of an algorithm in numerical analysis indicates how the error is propagated by the algorithm.

One commonly distinguishes between the relative error and the absolute error. The absolute error is the magnitude of the difference between the exact value and the approximation.

- a. ACTRAN
- b. ALGOR
- c. AUSM
- d. Approximation error

4. In infinitesimal calculus, a _____ is traditionally an infinitesimally small change in a variable. For example, if x is a variable, then a change in the value of x is often denoted Δx (or δx when this change is considered to be small.) The _____ dx represents such a change, but is infinitely small.

a. Local maximum
b. Dirichlet integral
c. The Method of Mechanical Theorems
d. Differential

5. In mathematics and its applications, _____ refers to finding the linear approximation to a function at a given point. In the study of dynamical systems, _____ is a method for assessing the local stability of an equilibrium point of a system of nonlinear differential equations or discrete dynamical systems. This method is used in fields such as engineering, physics, economics, and ecology.

a. Smooth function
b. Differentiation of trigonometric functions
c. Parametric derivative
d. Linearization

6. In calculus, a branch of mathematics, the _____ is a measurement of how a function changes when its input changes. Loosely speaking, a _____ can be thought of as how much a quantity is changing at some given point. For example, the _____ of the position (or distance) of a vehicle with respect to time is the instantaneous velocity (respectively, instantaneous speed) at which the vehicle is traveling.

The process of finding a _____ is called differentiation. The fundamental theorem of calculus states that differentiation is the reverse process to integration.

a. Stationary phase approximation
b. Semi-differentiability
c. Bounded function
d. Derivative

7. In mathematics, a _____ is a function which preserves the given order. This concept first arose in calculus, and was later generalized to the more abstract setting of order theory.

In calculus, a function f defined on a subset of the real numbers with real values is called monotonic (also monotonically increasing or non-decreasing), if for all x and y such that x >≤ y one has f(x) >≤ f(y), so f preserves the order.

a. Pseudo-differential operator
b. 15 theorem
c. Pettis integral
d. Monotonic function

8. In vector calculus, the _____ is an operator that measures the magnitude of a vector field's source or sink at a given point; the _____ of a vector field is a (signed) scalar. For example, consider air as it is heated or cooled. The relevant vector field for this example is the velocity of the moving air at a point.

a. Gradient theorem
b. Green's theorem
c. Triple product
d. Divergence

9. In vector calculus, the _____ Ostrogradskye;s theorem the _____ states that the outward flux of a vector field through a surface is equal to the triple integral of the divergence on the region inside the surface. Intuitively, it states that the sum of all sources minus the sum of all sinks gives the net flow out of a region.

a. Green's theorem
b. Divergence
c. Del
d. Divergence theorem

10. In probability theory and statistics, the _____ (or expectation value or mean and for continuous random variables with a density function it is the probability density -weighted integral of the possible values.

The term '_____' can be misleading.

- a. ALGOR
- b. Expected value
- c. ACTRAN
- d. AUSM

11. In calculus, the _____ states, roughly, that given a section of a smooth curve, there is at least one point on that section at which the derivative (slope) of the curve is equal (parallel) to the 'average' derivative of the section. It is used to prove theorems that make global conclusions about a function on an interval starting from local hypotheses about derivatives at points of the interval.

This theorem can be understood concretely by applying it to motion: If a car travels one hundred miles in one hour, so its average speed during that time was 100 miles per hour.

- a. Limits of integration
- b. Mean value theorem
- c. Hyperbolic angle
- d. Periodic function

12. Integration is an important concept in mathematics, specifically in the field of calculus and, more broadly, mathematical analysis. Given a function f of a real variable x and an interval [a, b] of the real line, the _____

$$\int_a^b f(x)\,dx ,$$

is defined informally to be the net signed area of the region in the xy-plane bounded by the graph of f, the x-axis, and the vertical lines x = a and x = b.

The term '_____' may also refer to the notion of antiderivative, a function F whose derivative is the given function f.

- a. Integrand
- b. Integral test for convergence
- c. Indefinite integral
- d. Integral

13. _____ is a way of expressing knowledge or belief that an event will occur or has occurred. In mathematics the concept has been given an exact meaning in _____ theory, that is used extensively in such areas of study as mathematics, statistics, finance, gambling, science, and philosophy to draw conclusions about the likelihood of potential events and the underlying mechanics of complex systems.

The word _____ does not have a consistent direct definition.

- a. Linear regression
- b. Normal distribution
- c. Discrete probability distributions
- d. Probability

Chapter 4. ADDITIONAL APPLICATIONS OF THE DERIVATIVE

14. In mathematics, an _____, is the apparent shape of a circle viewed obliquely from outside it, as distinct from a hyperbola which is the shape seen from inside. It is the finite or bounded case of a conic section as a shape cut in a cone by a plane, the unbounded cases being the parabola, which like the _____ remains connected, and the hyperbola, which separates into two connected components or branches.

Equivalently an _____ can be defined as the locus of points, or path traced out, in a plane such that the sum of the distances from the moving point to two fixed points remains constant.

    a. ALGOR   b. AUSM
    c. ACTRAN   d. Ellipse

15. In mathematics and computer science, the floor and ceiling functions map a real number to the next smallest or next largest integer. More precisely, floor(x) is the largest integer not greater than x and ceiling(x) is the smallest integer not less than x.

The _____ is also called the greatest integer or entier function, and the floor of a nonnegative x may be called the integral part or integral value of x. Computer languages (other than APL) commonly use ENTIER(x) (Algol), floor(x), or int(x) (C and C++).

    a. Hyperbolic functions   b. Multiplicative inverse
    c. Hyperbolic tangent   d. Floor function

16. A real-valued function f defined on the real line is said to have a _____ point at the point $x^{>*}$, if there exists some $>\varepsilon > 0$, such that $f(x^{>*}) >\geq f(x)$ when $|x >- x^{>*}| < >\varepsilon$. The value of the function at this point is called maximum of the function.

On a graph of a function, its local maxima will look like the tops of hills.

    a. Standard part function   b. Test for Divergence
    c. Local maximum   d. Racetrack principle

17. In a totally ordered set all elements are mutually comparable, so such a set can have at most one minimal element and at most one maximal element. Then, due to mutual comparability, the minimal element will also be the least element and the maximal element will also be the greatest element. Thus in a totally ordered set we can simply use the terms minimum and _____.

    a. Racetrack principle   b. Nth term
    c. Leibniz rule   d. Maximum

18. In a totally ordered set all elements are mutually comparable, so such a set can have at most one minimal element and at most one maximal element. Then, due to mutual comparability, the minimal element will also be the least element and the maximal element will also be the greatest element. Thus in a totally ordered set we can simply use the terms _____ and maximum.

    a. Minimum   b. Maximum
    c. Nth term   d. Ghosts of departed quantities

19. In mathematics, the interior of a set S consists of all points of S that are intuitively 'not on the edge of S'. A point that is in the interior of S is an _____ of S.

Chapter 4. ADDITIONAL APPLICATIONS OF THE DERIVATIVE

The exterior of a set is the interior of its complement; it consists of the points that are not in the set or its boundary.

a. ALGOR
b. Interior point
c. AUSM
d. ACTRAN

20. Continuous functions are of utmost importance in mathematics and applications. However, not all functions are continuous. If a function is not continuous at a point in its domain, one says that it has a _____ there. The set of all points of _____ of a function may be a discrete set, a dense set, or even the entire domain of the function.

a. Vector
b. Discontinuity
c. BDDC
d. 15 theorem

21. In mathematics, a _____ (or critical number) is a point on the domain of a function where:

- one dimension: the derivative (or slope of the line when visualized) is equal to zero or a point where the function ceases to be differentiable.
- in general: there are two distinct concepts: either the derivative (Jacobian) vanishes, or it is not of full rank (or, in either case, the function is not differentiable); these agree in one dimension.

Note that in one dimension, a critical value or critical number x of function f is the domain element at which the derivative is zero or undefined, whereas the associated ordered pair (x, y) is the _____. In higher dimensions a critical value is in the range whereas a _____ is in the domain.

There are two situations in which a point becomes a _____ of a function of one variable. The first of which is that the value of the first derivative is equal to zero.

a. Differentiation operator
b. Total derivative
c. Multivariable calculus
d. Critical point

22. In calculus, the _____ determines whether a given critical point of a function is a maximum, a minimum, or neither.

Suppose that f is a function and we want to determine if f has a maximum or minimum at x. If f is increasing to the left of x and decreasing to the right of x, then x is a local maximum of f.

a. First derivative test
b. Continuous function
c. Test for Divergence
d. Partial sum

23. In mathematics, _____ and minima, known collectively as extrema, are the largest value (maximum) or smallest value (minimum), that a function takes in a point either within a given neighbourhood (local extremum) or on the function domain in its entirety (global extremum.)

Throughout, a point refers to an input (x), while a value refers to an output (y): one distinguishing between the maximum value and the point (or points) at which it occurs.

A real-valued function f defined on the real line is said to have a local maximum point at the point x*, if there exists some ε > 0, such that f(x*) ≥ f(x) when |x − x*| < ε.

- a. Related rates
- b. Leibniz formula
- c. Racetrack principle
- d. Maxima

24. In metric topology and related fields of mathematics, a set U is called _____ if, intuitively speaking, starting from any point x in U one can move by a small amount in any direction and still be in the set U. In other words, the distance between any point x in U and the edge of U is always greater than zero.

As an example, consider the _____ interval (0, 1) consisting of all real numbers x with 0 < x < 1. Here, the topology is the usual topology on the real line. We can look at this in two ways.

- a. ACTRAN
- b. AUSM
- c. ALGOR
- d. Open

25. In calculus and other branches of mathematical analysis, an _____ is an algebraic expression obtained in the context of limits. Limits involving algebraic operations are often performed by replacing subexpressions by their limits; if the expression obtained after this substitution does not give enough information to determine the original limit, it is known as an _____. The indeterminate forms include 0^0, $0/0$, 1^∞, $\infty - \infty$, ∞/∞, $0\times\infty$, and ∞^0.

- a. ALGOR
- b. AUSM
- c. ACTRAN
- d. Indeterminate form

26. In mathematics, a (topological) _____ is defined as follows: let I be an interval of real numbers (i.e. a non-empty connected subset of $\mathbb{R}$); then a _____ γ is a continuous mapping $\gamma : I \to X$, where X is a topological space. The _____ γ is said to be simple if it is injective, i.e. if for all x, y in I, we have $\gamma(x) = \gamma(y) \implies x = y$. If I is a closed bounded interval $[a, b]$, we also allow the possibility $\gamma(a) = \gamma(b)$ (this convention makes it possible to talk about closed simple _____.)

- a. Closed curve
- b. Prolate cycloid
- c. Curve
- d. Tractrix

27. A _____ is perfectly round geometrical object in three-dimensional space, such as the shape of a round ball. Like a circle in two dimensions, a perfect _____ is completely symmetrical around its center, with all points on the surface lying the same distance r from the center point. This distance r is known as the radius of the _____.

- a. Tangent line
- b. Minimal surface
- c. North pole
- d. Sphere

28. The _____ of any solid, liquid, plasma, vacuum or theoretical object is how much three-dimensional space it occupies, often quantified numerically. One-dimensional figures (such as lines) and two-dimensional shapes (such as squares) are assigned zero _____ in the three-dimensional space. _____ is commonly presented in units such as mL or cm^3 (milliliters or cubic centimeters.)

- a. Vector potential
- b. Volume
- c. Dirac equation
- d. Klein-Gordon equation

Chapter 4. ADDITIONAL APPLICATIONS OF THE DERIVATIVE

29. Let f be a differentiable function, and let f'(x) be its derivative. The derivative of f'(x) (if it has one) is written f''(x) and is called the _____ of f. Similarly, the derivative of a _____, if it exists, is written f'''(x) and is called the third derivative of f.

    a. Stationary phase approximation
    b. Second derivative
    c. Slant asymptote
    d. Vertical asymptote

30. In calculus, a branch of mathematics, the _____ is a criterion often useful for determining whether a given stationary point of a function is a local maximum or a local minimum.

The test states: If the function f is twice differentiable at a stationary point x, meaning that $f'(x) = 0$, then:

- If $f''(x) < 0$ then f has a local maximum at x.
- If $f''(x) > 0$ then f has a local minimum at x.
- If $f''(x) = 0$, the _____ says nothing about the point x, has a possible inflection point.

In the last case, the function may have a local maximum or minimum there, but the function is sufficiently 'flat' that this is undetected by the second derivative. In this case one has to examine the third derivative. Such an example is f(x) = x⁴.

    a. Linearity of differentiation
    b. Stationary point
    c. Symmetric derivative
    d. Second derivative test

31. In mathematics, a function f defined on some set X with real or complex values is a _____ function, if the set of its values is _____. In other words, there exists a number M>0 such that

$$|f(x)| \leq M$$

for all x in X.

Sometimes, if $f(x) \leq A$ for all x in X, then the function is said to be _____ above by A.

    a. Stationary phase approximation
    b. Differential coefficient
    c. Bounded
    d. Concave upwards

32. In mathematics, a real-valued function f defined on an interval (or on any convex subset of some vector space) is called convex, _____, concave up or convex cup, if for any two points x and y in its domain C and any t in [0,1], we have

$$f(tx + (1-t)y) \leq tf(x) + (1-t)f(y).$$

Convex function on an interval.

In other words, a function is convex if and only if its epigraph (the set of points lying on or above the graph) is a convex set.

Pictorially, a function is called 'convex' if the function lies below the straight line segment connecting two points, for any two points in the interval.

A function is called strictly convex if

$$f(tx + (1-t)y) < tf(x) + (1-t)f(y)$$

for any t in (0,1) and $x \neq y$.

A function f is said to be concave if − f is convex.

- a. Third derivative
- b. Vertical asymptote
- c. Mountain pass theorem
- d. Concave upwards

33. In differential calculus, an inflection point, or _____ (or inflexion) is a point on a curve at which the curvature changes sign. The curve changes from being concave upwards (positive curvature) to concave downwards (negative curvature), or vice versa. If one imagines driving a vehicle along the curve, it is a point at which the steering-wheel is momentarily 'straight', being turned from left to right or vice versa.
- a. Logarithmic derivative
- b. Derivative of a constant
- c. Point of inflection
- d. Lin-Tsien equation

34. _____ is any physical or virtual entity that is owned by an individual or jointly by a group of individuals. An owner of _____ has the right to consume, sell, rent, mortgage, transfer and exchange his or her _____. Important widely-recognized types of _____ include real _____, personal _____ (other physical possessions), and intellectual _____ (rights over artistic creations, inventions, etc.), although the latter is not always as widely recognized or enforced.
- a. BDDC
- b. 15 theorem
- c. BIBO stability
- d. Property

35. In mathematics, a _____ is an ordered list of objects (or events). Like a set, it contains members (also called elements or terms), and the number of terms (possibly infinite) is called the length of the _____. Unlike a set, order matters, and the exact same elements can appear multiple times at different positions in the _____.
- a. Y-intercept
- b. Slope
- c. 15 theorem
- d. Sequence

36. Cantor defined two kinds of _____ numbers, the ordinal numbers and the cardinal numbers. Ordinal numbers may be identified with well-ordered sets, or counting carried on to any stopping point, including points after an _____ number have already been counted. Generalizing finite and the ordinary _____ sequences which are maps from the positive integers leads to mappings from ordinal numbers, and transfinite sequences.
- a. AUSM
- b. ACTRAN
- c. ALGOR
- d. Infinite

Chapter 4. ADDITIONAL APPLICATIONS OF THE DERIVATIVE

37. The terms of the series are often produced according to a certain rule, such as by a formula, by an algorithm, by a sequence of measurements, or even by a random number generator. As there are an infinite number of terms, this notion is often called an _____. Unlike finite summations, series need tools from mathematical analysis to be fully understood and manipulated.

    a. Infinite series   b. Extreme value
    c. Extreme Value Theorem   d. Integration by substitution

38. In mathematics, the concept of a '_____' is used to describe the behavior of a function as its argument or input either 'gets close' to some point, or as the argument becomes arbitrarily large; or the behavior of a sequence's elements as their index increases indefinitely. Limits are used in calculus and other branches of mathematical analysis to define derivatives and continuity.

In formulas, _____ is usually abbreviated as lim

    a. 15 theorem   b. Limit
    c. BIBO stability   d. BDDC

39. The _____ of a biological species in an environment is the population size of the species that the environment can sustain in the long term, given the food, habitat, water and other necessities available in the environment. For the human population, more complex variables such as sanitation and medical care are sometimes considered as part of the necessary infrastructure.

As population density increases, birth rate often increases and death rate typically decreases.

    a. BIBO stability   b. 15 theorem
    c. BDDC   d. Carrying capacity

40. The concept of _____ in mathematics evolved from the concept of _____ in physics. The nth _____ of a real-valued function f(x) of a real variable about a value c is

$$\mu'_n = \int_{-\infty}^{\infty} (x-c)^n f(x)\, dx.$$

It is possible to define moments for random variables in a more general fashion than moments for real values. See Moments in metric spaces.

    a. Median   b. Moment
    c. Geometric mean   d. Poisson distribution

41. In geometry, the _____ (or simply the tangent) to a curve at a given point is the straight line that 'just touches' the curve at that point (in the sense explained more precisely below.) As it passes through the point of tangency, the _____ is 'going in the same direction' as the curve, and in this sense it is the best straight-line approximation to the curve at that point. The same definition applies to space curves and curves in n-dimensional Euclidean space.

a. Minimal surface
c. North pole
b. Lie derivative
d. Tangent line

42. In mathematics, the _____ for convergence is a method used to test infinite series of non-negative terms for convergence. An early form of the test of convergence was developed in India by Madhava in the 14th century, and by his followers at the Kerala School. In Europe, it was later developed by Maclaurin and Cauchy and is sometimes known as the Maclaurin-Cauchy test.

a. ACTRAN
c. ALGOR
b. AUSM
d. Integral test

Chapter 5. S THE INTEGRAL

1. The _____ specifies the relationship between the two central operations of calculus, differentiation and integration.

The first part of the theorem, sometimes called the first _____, shows that an indefinite integration can be reversed by a differentiation.

The second part, sometimes called the second _____, allows one to compute the definite integral of a function by using any one of its infinitely many antiderivatives.

- a. Periodic function
- b. Leibniz formula
- c. Limits of integration
- d. Fundamental theorem of calculus

2. In mathematics, the _____ are analogs of the ordinary trigonometric or circular functions. The basic _____ are the hyperbolic sine 'sinh', and the hyperbolic cosine 'cosh', from which are derived the hyperbolic tangent 'tanh', etc., in analogy to the derived trigonometric functions. The inverse _____ are the area hyperbolic sine 'arsinh' (also called 'asinh', or sometimes by the misnomer of 'arcsinh') and so on.

- a. Hyperbolic cosine
- b. Multiplicative inverse
- c. Signum function
- d. Hyperbolic functions

3. In calculus, an _____, primitive or indefinite integral of a function f is a function F whose derivative is equal to f, i.e., F >' = f. The process of solving for antiderivatives is antidifferentiation (or indefinite integration.) Antiderivatives are related to definite integrals through the fundamental theorem of calculus: the definite integral of a function over an interval is equal to the difference between the values of an _____ evaluated at the endpoints of the interval.

- a. Order of integration
- b. Integrand
- c. Indefinite integral
- d. Antiderivative

4. A _____ officer is an officer of high military rank. The term or equivalent is used by nearly every country in the world. _____ can be used as a generic term for all grades of _____ officer, or it can specifically refer to a single rank that is just called _____.

- a. BIBO stability
- b. BDDC
- c. 15 theorem
- d. General

5. In calculus, an antiderivative, primitive or _____ of a function f is a function F whose derivative is equal to f, i.e., F ' = f. The process of solving for antiderivatives is antidifferentiation (or indefinite integration.) Antiderivatives are related to definite integrals through the fundamental theorem of calculus: the definite integral of a function over an interval is equal to the difference between the values of an antiderivative evaluated at the endpoints of the interval.

- a. Integration by parts operator
- b. Arc length
- c. Indefinite integral
- d. Integral test for convergence

6. In infinitesimal calculus, a _____ is traditionally an infinitesimally small change in a variable. For example, if x is a variable, then a change in the value of x is often denoted Δx (or δx when this change is considered to be small.) The _____ dx represents such a change, but is infinitely small.

- a. Differential
- b. Dirichlet integral
- c. Local maximum
- d. The Method of Mechanical Theorems

7. Integration is an important concept in mathematics, specifically in the field of calculus and, more broadly, mathematical analysis. Given a function f of a real variable x and an interval [a, b] of the real line, the _____

$$\int_a^b f(x)\,dx,$$

is defined informally to be the net signed area of the region in the xy-plane bounded by the graph of f, the x-axis, and the vertical lines x = a and x = b.

The term '_____' may also refer to the notion of antiderivative, a function F whose derivative is the given function f.

    a. Integral
    b. Integrand
    c. Indefinite integral
    d. Integral test for convergence

8. In mathematics, the hyperbolic functions are analogs of the ordinary trigonometric functions. The basic hyperbolic functions are the hyperbolic sine 'sinh', and the _____ 'cosh', from which are derived the hyperbolic tangent 'tanh', etc., in analogy to the derived trigonometric functions. The inverse hyperbolic functions are the area hyperbolic sine 'arsinh' (also called 'asinh', or sometimes by the misnomer of 'arcsinh') and so on.

    a. Square root function
    b. Step function
    c. Hyperbolic tangent
    d. Hyperbolic cosine

9. In mathematics and its applications, a _____ system is a system for assigning an n-tuple of numbers or scalars to each point in an n-dimensional space. This concept is part of the theory of manifolds. 'Scalars' in many cases means real numbers, but, depending on context, can mean complex numbers or elements of some other commutative ring.

    a. Cylindrical coordinate system
    b. Spherical coordinate system
    c. 15 theorem
    d. Coordinate

10. _____ (including exponential decay) occurs when the growth rate of a mathematical function is proportional to the function's current value. In the case of a discrete domain of definition with equal intervals it is also called geometric growth or geometric decay (the function values form a geometric progression.)

_____ is said to follow an exponential law; the simple-_____ model is known as the Malthusian growth model.

    a. Isomonodromic deformation
    b. Inseparable differential equation
    c. Oscillating
    d. Exponential growth

11. In mathematics, particularly in complex analysis, a _____, first studied by and named after Bernhard Riemann, is a one-dimensional complex manifold. Riemann surfaces can be thought of as 'deformed versions' of the complex plane: locally near every point they look like patches of the complex plane, but the global topology can be quite different. For example, they can look like a sphere or a torus or a couple of sheets glued together.

    a. Lacunary value
    b. Riemann surface
    c. Radius of convergence
    d. Pole

12. In mathematics, a _____ to an ordinary or partial differential equation is a function for which the derivatives appearing in the equation may not all exist but which is nonetheless deemed to satisfy the equation in some precisely defined sense. There are many different definitions of _____, appropriate for different classes of equations. One of the most important is based on the notion of distributions.
   a. Conserved quantity
   b. Singular perturbation
   c. Structural stability
   d. Weak solution

13. In mathematics, in the field of differential equations, an initial value problem is an ordinary differential equation together with specified value, called the _____, of the unknown function at a given point in the domain of the solution. In physics or other sciences, modeling a system frequently amounts to solving an initial value problem; in this context, the differential equation is an evolution equation specifying how, given initial conditions, the system will evolve with time.

An initial value problem is a differential equation

$$y'(t) = f(t, y(t)) \quad \text{with} \quad f : \mathbb{R} \times \mathbb{R} \to \mathbb{R}$$

together with a point in the domain of f

$$(t_0, y_0) \in \mathbb{R} \times \mathbb{R},$$

called the _____.

   a. ACTRAN
   b. ALGOR
   c. AUSM
   d. Initial condition

14. In physics, and more specifically kinematics, _____ is the change in velocity over time. Because velocity is a vector, it can change in two ways: a change in magnitude and/or a change in direction. In one dimension, _____ is the rate at which something speeds up or slows down.
   a. ALGOR
   b. AUSM
   c. ACTRAN
   d. Acceleration

15. In physics, _____ is defined as the rate of change of position. it is vector physical quantity; both speed and direction are required to define it. In the SI (metric) system, it is measured in meters per second: (m/s) or ms^{-1}.
   a. 15 theorem
   b. BIBO stability
   c. BDDC
   d. Velocity

16. In vector calculus, the _____ of a scalar field is a vector field which points in the direction of the greatest rate of increase of the scalar field, and whose magnitude is the greatest rate of change.

A generalization of the _____ for functions on a Euclidean space which have values in another Euclidean space is the Jacobian. A further generalization for a function from one Banach space to another is the Fréchet derivative.

a. Symmetric derivative
b. Smooth function
c. Lin-Tsien equation
d. Gradient

17. _____ is the addition of a set of numbers; the result is their sum or total. An interim or present total of a _____ process is termed the running total. The 'numbers' to be summed may be natural numbers, complex numbers, matrices, or still more complicated objects.

a. Summation
b. BIBO stability
c. BDDC
d. 15 theorem

18. In elementary mathematics, physics, and engineering, a _____ is a geometric object that has both a magnitude (or length), direction and sense, (i.e., orientation along the given direction.) A _____ is frequently represented by a line segment with a definite direction, or graphically as an arrow, connecting an initial point A with a terminal point B, and denoted by

The magnitude of the _____ is the length of the segment and the direction characterizes the displacement of B relative to A: how much one should move the point A to 'carry' it to the point B.

Many algebraic operations on real numbers have close analogues for vectors.

a. Linear partial differential operator
b. BDDC
c. Vector
d. 15 theorem

19. In mathematics a _____ is a construction in vector calculus which associates a vector to every point in a (locally) Euclidean space.

Vector fields are often used in physics to model, for example, the speed and direction of a moving fluid throughout space, or the strength and direction of some force, such as the magnetic or gravitational force, as it changes from point to point.

In the rigorous mathematical treatment, (tangent) vector fields are defined on manifolds as sections of a manifold's tangent bundle.

a. BDDC
b. 15 theorem
c. Vector field
d. BIBO stability

20. The _____ of a biological species in an environment is the population size of the species that the environment can sustain in the long term, given the food, habitat, water and other necessities available in the environment. For the human population, more complex variables such as sanitation and medical care are sometimes considered as part of the necessary infrastructure.

As population density increases, birth rate often increases and death rate typically decreases.

a. BIBO stability
c. BDDC
b. 15 theorem
d. Carrying capacity

21. In mathematics, the concept of a '_____' is used to describe the behavior of a function as its argument or input either 'gets close' to some point, or as the argument becomes arbitrarily large; or the behavior of a sequence's elements as their index increases indefinitely. Limits are used in calculus and other branches of mathematical analysis to define derivatives and continuity.

In formulas, _____ is usually abbreviated as lim

   a. BIBO stability
   c. 15 theorem
   b. BDDC
   d. Limit

22. A _____ is a special kind of space curve, i.e. a smooth curve in three-space. As a mental image of a _____ one may take the spring (although the spring is not a curve, and so is technically not a _____, it does give a convenient mental picture.) A _____ is characterised by the fact that the tangent line at any point makes a constant angle with a fixed line.
   a. BIBO stability
   c. 15 theorem
   b. BDDC
   d. Helix

23. In mathematics, a (topological) _____ is defined as follows: let I be an interval of real numbers (i.e. a non-empty connected subset of $\mathbb{R}$); then a _____ γ is a continuous mapping $\gamma : I \to X$, where X is a topological space. The _____ γ is said to be simple if it is injective, i.e. if for all x, y in I, we have $\gamma(x) = \gamma(y) \implies x = y$. If I is a closed bounded interval $[a, b]$, we also allow the possibility $\gamma(a) = \gamma(b)$ (this convention makes it possible to talk about closed simple _____.)
   a. Prolate cycloid
   c. Tractrix
   b. Closed curve
   d. Curve

24. A _____ is a mathematical equation for an unknown function of one or several variables that relates the values of the function itself and of its derivatives of various orders. they play a prominent role in engineering, physics, economics and other disciplines.

A simplified real world example of a _____ is modeling the acceleration of a ball falling through the air (considering only gravity and air resistance.)

   a. Phase line
   c. Differential equation
   b. Caloric polynomial
   d. Structural stability

25. In mathematics, a _____ is a method for approximating the total area underneath a curve on a graph, otherwise known as an integral. It may also be used to define the integration operation.

Consider a function $f: D \rightarrow \mathbf{R}$, where D is a subset of the real numbers $\mathbf{R}$, and let $I = [a, b]$ be a closed interval contained in D. A finite set of points $\{x_0, x_1, x_2, \ldots x_n\}$ such that $a = x_0 < x_1 < x_2 \ldots < x_n = b$ creates a partition

$$P = \{[x_0, x_1), [x_1, x_2), \ldots [x_{n-1}, x_n]\}$$

of I.

    a. Solid of revolution   b. Signed measure
    c. Risch algorithm   d. Riemann sum

26.   In mathematics, an _____ is a function whose integral exists. Unless specifically stated, the integral in question is usually the Lebesgue integral. Otherwise, one can say that the function is 'Riemann-integrable' (i.e., its Riemann integral exists), 'Henstock-Kurzweil-integrable,' etc.

    a. AUSM   b. Integrable function
    c. ALGOR   d. ACTRAN

27.   If a function has an integral, it is said to be integrable. The function for which the integral is calculated is called the _____. The region over which a function is being integrated is called the domain of integration.

    a. Integral test for convergence   b. Integration by parts
    c. Order of integration   d. Integrand

28.   In mathematics, a _____ is an ordered list of objects (or events). Like a set, it contains members (also called elements or terms), and the number of terms (possibly infinite) is called the length of the _____. Unlike a set, order matters, and the exact same elements can appear multiple times at different positions in the _____.

    a. Slope   b. 15 theorem
    c. Y-intercept   d. Sequence

29.   In acoustics and telecommunication, a _____ of a wave is a component frequency of the signal that is an integer multiple of the fundamental frequency. For example, if the fundamental frequency is f, the harmonics have frequencies f, 2f, 3f, 4f, etc. The harmonics have the property that they are all periodic at the fundamental frequency, therefore the sum of harmonics is also periodic at that frequency.

    a. 15 theorem   b. BDDC
    c. BIBO stability   d. Harmonic

30.   In mathematics, the _____ is the infinite series

$$\sum_{k=1}^{\infty} \frac{1}{k} = 1 + \frac{1}{2} + \frac{1}{3} + \frac{1}{4} + \cdots.$$

Its name derives from the concept of overtones, or harmonics, in music: the wavelengths of the overtones of a vibrating string are 1/2, 1/3, 1/4, etc., of the string's fundamental wavelength. Every term of the series after the first is the harmonic mean of the neighboring terms; the term harmonic mean likewise derives from music.

The _____ diverges to infinity, albeit rather slowly (the first 10^{43} terms sum to less than 100 .)

    a. 15 theorem
    b. BIBO stability
    c. BDDC
    d. Harmonic series

31. _____ is the long dimension of any object. The _____ of a thing is the distance between its ends, its linear extent as measured from end to end. This may be distinguished from height, which is vertical extent, and width or breadth, which are the distance from side to side, measuring across the object at right angles to the _____.

    a. BDDC
    b. BIBO stability
    c. 15 theorem
    d. Length

32. The _____ of a quantity whose value decreases with time is the interval required for the quantity to decay to half of its initial value. The concept originated in describing how long it takes atoms to undergo radioactive decay but also applies in a wide variety of other situations.

The term '_____' dates to 1907.

    a. 15 theorem
    b. BIBO stability
    c. Half-life
    d. BDDC

33. In mathematics, an _____ is an infinite series of the form

$$\sum_{n=0}^{\infty} (-1)^n a_n,$$

with $a_n \geq 0$ (or $a_n \leq 0$) for all n. A finite sum of this kind is an alternating sum. An _____ converges if the terms a_n converge to 0 monotonically.

    a. Infinite series
    b. Uniform convergence
    c. Extreme value
    d. Alternating series

34. The _____ is a method used to prove that infinite series of terms converge. It was discovered by Gottfried Leibniz and is sometimes known as Leibniz's test or the Leibniz criterion.

A series of the form

$$\sum_{n=1}^{\infty} (-1)^n a_n$$

where all the a_n are positive or 0, is called an alternating series.

a. Eisenstein series
b. Absolute convergence
c. ACTRAN
d. Alternating series test

35. In mathematics, in the field of differential equations, an _____ is an ordinary differential equation together with specified value, called the initial condition, of the unknown function at a given point in the domain of the solution. In physics or other sciences, modeling a system frequently amounts to solving an _____; in this context, the differential equation is an evolution equation specifying how, given initial conditions, the system will evolve with time.

An _____ is a differential equation

$$y'(t) = f(t, y(t)) \quad \text{with} \quad f : \mathbb{R} \times \mathbb{R} \to \mathbb{R}$$

together with a point in the domain of f

$$(t_0, y_0) \in \mathbb{R} \times \mathbb{R},$$

called the initial condition.

a. ALGOR
b. AUSM
c. ACTRAN
d. Initial value problem

36. In number theory, the _____ describes the asymptotic distribution of the prime numbers. The _____ gives a rough description of how the primes are distributed.

Roughly speaking, the _____ states that if you randomly select a number nearby some large number N, the chance of it being prime is about 1 / ln(N), where ln(N) denotes the natural logarithm of N. For example, near N = 10,000, about one in nine numbers is prime, whereas near N = 1,000,000,000, only one in every 21 numbers is prime.

a. Prime-counting function
b. Twin prime conjecture
c. Prime number theorem
d. Large sieve

37. Trigonometry is a branch of mathematics that deals with triangles, particularly those plane triangles in which one angle has 90 degrees (right triangles.) Trigonometry deals with relationships between the sides and the angles of triangles and with the _____ functions, which describe those relationships.

Trigonometry has applications in both pure mathematics and in applied mathematics, where it is essential in many branches of science and technology.

a. Sine
b. Trigonometric
c. Trigonometric integrals
d. Trigonometric functions

38. In mathematics, the _____ are a family of integrals which involve trigonometric functions. A number of the basic _____ are discussed at the list of integrals of trigonometric functions.

The different sine integral definitions are:

$$\mathrm{Si}(x) = \int_0^x \frac{\sin t}{t}\, dt$$

$$\mathrm{si}(x) = -\int_x^\infty \frac{\sin t}{t}\, dt$$

Si(x) is the primitive of sinx / x which is zero for x = 0; si(x) is the primitive of sinx / x which is zero for $x = \infty$.

- a. Trigonometric functions
- b. Trigonometric
- c. Trigonometric integrals
- d. Sine

39. In mathematics, a series (or sometimes also an integral) is said to converge absolutely if the sum (or integral) of the absolute value of the summand or integrand is finite.

More precisely, a real or complex-valued series $\sum_{n=0}^{\infty} a_n$ is said to converge absolutely if $\sum_{n=0}^{\infty} |a_n| < \infty$.

_____ is vitally important to the study of infinite series because on the one hand, it is strong enough that such series retain certain basic properties of finite sums -- the most important ones being rearrangement of the terms and convergence of products of two infinite series -- that are unfortunately not possessed by all convergent series. On the other hand _____ is weak enough to occur very often in practice.

- a. ACTRAN
- b. Absolute convergence
- c. Alternating series test
- d. Eisenstein series

40. In a totally ordered set all elements are mutually comparable, so such a set can have at most one minimal element and at most one maximal element. Then, due to mutual comparability, the minimal element will also be the least element and the maximal element will also be the greatest element. Thus in a totally ordered set we can simply use the terms minimum and _____.

- a. Nth term
- b. Racetrack principle
- c. Leibniz rule
- d. Maximum

41. In a totally ordered set all elements are mutually comparable, so such a set can have at most one minimal element and at most one maximal element. Then, due to mutual comparability, the minimal element will also be the least element and the maximal element will also be the greatest element. Thus in a totally ordered set we can simply use the terms _____ and maximum.

- a. Nth term
- b. Ghosts of departed quantities
- c. Maximum
- d. Minimum

Chapter 5. S THE INTEGRAL

42. In computer science and information science, _____ could also be a method or an algorithm. Again, an example will illustrate: There are systems of counting, as with Roman numerals, and various systems for filing papers, or catalogues, and various library systems, of which the Dewey Decimal _____ is an example. This still fits with the definition of components which are connected together (in this case in order to facilitate the flow of information.)
- a. BDDC
- b. BIBO stability
- c. System
- d. 15 theorem

43. In mathematics, a _____ (in one variable) is an infinite series of the form

$$f(x) = \sum_{n=0}^{\infty} a_n (x-c)^n = a_0 + a_1(x-c)^1 + a_2(x-c)^2 + a_3(x-c)^3 + \cdots$$

where a_n represents the coefficient of the nth term, c is a constant, and x varies around c (for this reason one sometimes speaks of the series as being centered at c

In many situations c is equal to zero, for instance when considering a Maclaurin series.

- a. Differential coefficient
- b. Differential calculus
- c. Stationary phase approximation
- d. Power series

44. In calculus, a branch of mathematics, the _____ is a measurement of how a function changes when its input changes. Loosely speaking, a _____ can be thought of as how much a quantity is changing at some given point. For example, the _____ of the position (or distance) of a vehicle with respect to time is the instantaneous velocity (respectively, instantaneous speed) at which the vehicle is traveling.

The process of finding a _____ is called differentiation. The fundamental theorem of calculus states that differentiation is the reverse process to integration.

- a. Stationary phase approximation
- b. Bounded function
- c. Semi-differentiability
- d. Derivative

45. _____ is used to describe the steepness, incline, gradient, or grade of a straight line. A higher _____ value indicates a steeper incline. The _____ is defined as the ratio of the 'rise' divided by the 'run' between two points on a line, or in other words, the ratio of the altitude change to the horizontal distance between any two points on the line.
- a. Sequence
- b. Slope
- c. Y-intercept
- d. 15 theorem

46. In mathematics, a _____ (or direction field) is a graphical representation of the solutions of a first-order differential equation. It is achieved without solving the differential equation analytically, and thence it is useful. The representation may be used to qualitatively visualise solutions, or to numerically approximate them.
- a. Leibniz function
- b. Visual Calculus
- c. Continuous function
- d. Slope field

Chapter 5. S THE INTEGRAL

47. The _____ in some data is the discrepancy between an exact value and some approximation to it. An _____ can occur because

    1. the measurement of the data is not precise (due to the instruments), or
    2. approximations are used instead of the real data (e.g., 3.14 instead of π.)

In the mathematical field of numerical analysis, the numerical stability of an algorithm in numerical analysis indicates how the error is propagated by the algorithm.

One commonly distinguishes between the relative error and the absolute error. The absolute error is the magnitude of the difference between the exact value and the approximation.

    a. ACTRAN   b. ALGOR
    c. AUSM   d. Approximation error

48. The function difference divided by the point difference is known as the _____, it is also known as Newton's quotient):

$$\frac{\Delta F(P)}{\Delta P} = \frac{F(P + \Delta P) - F(P)}{\Delta P} = \frac{\nabla F(P + \Delta P)}{\Delta P}.$$

If ΔP is infinitesimal, then the _____ is a derivative, otherwise it is a divided difference:

$$\text{If } |\Delta P| = iota: \quad \frac{\Delta F(P)}{\Delta P} = \frac{dF(P)}{dP} = F'(P) = G(P);$$

$$\text{If } |\Delta P| > iota: \quad \frac{\Delta F(P)}{\Delta P} = \frac{DF(P)}{DP} = F[P, P + \Delta P].$$

Regardless if ΔP is infinitesimal or finite, there is (at least--in the case of the derivative--theoretically) a point range, where the boundaries are P ± (.5)ΔP (depending on the orientation--ΔF(P), δF(P) or ∇F(P)):

    LB = Lower Boundary; UB = Upper Boundary;

Anyone familiar with derivatives knows that they can be regarded as functions themselves, harboring their own derivatives. Thus each function is home to sequential degrees ('higher orders') of derivation, or differentiation. This property can be generalized to all difference quotients.As this sequencing requires a corresponding boundary splintering, it is practical to break up the point range into smaller, equi-sized sections, with each section being marked by an intermediary point ('P_i''), where LB = P_0 and UB = P_{A_n}, the nth point, equaling the degree/order:

LB = P_0 = P_0 + $0\Delta_1 P$ = P_{A_m} - $(Åf-0)\Delta_1 P$; P_1 = P_0 + $1\Delta_1 P$ = P_{A_m} - $(Åf-1)\Delta_1 P$; P_2 = P_0 + $2\Delta_1 P$ = P_{A_m} - $(Åf-2)\Delta_1 P$; P_3 = P_0 + $3\Delta_1 P$ = P_{A_m} - $(Åf-3)\Delta_1 P$; ↓↓↓↓ P_{A_m-3} = P_0 + $(Åf-3)\Delta_1 P$ = P_{A_m} - $3\Delta_1 P$; P_{A_m-2} = P_0 + $(Åf-2)\Delta_1 P$ = P_{A_m} - $2\Delta_1 P$; P_{A_m-1} = P_0 + $(Åf-1)\Delta_1 P$ = P_{A_m} - $1\Delta_1 P$; UB = P_{A_m-0} = P_0 + $(Åf-0)\Delta_1 P$ = P_{A_m} - $0\Delta_1 P$ = P_{A_m};

$\Delta P = \Delta_1 P = P_1 - P_0 = P_2 - P_1 = P_3 - P_2 = \ldots$

a. Continuously differentiable
b. Directional derivative
c. Notation for differentiation
d. Difference quotient

Chapter 6. APPLICATIONS OF THE INTEGRAL

1. In calculus, the _____ is a theorem regarding the limit of a function.

The _____ is a technical result which is very important in proofs in calculus and mathematical analysis. It is typically used to confirm the limit of a function via comparison with two other functions whose limits are known or easily computed.

   a. Limit of a sequence
   b. Table of limits
   c. 15 theorem
   d. Squeeze Theorem

2. The _____ of any solid, liquid, plasma, vacuum or theoretical object is how much three-dimensional space it occupies, often quantified numerically. One-dimensional figures (such as lines) and two-dimensional shapes (such as squares) are assigned zero _____ in the three-dimensional space. _____ is commonly presented in units such as mL or cm^3 (milliliters or cubic centimeters.)

   a. Volume
   b. Dirac equation
   c. Klein-Gordon equation
   d. Vector potential

3. A _____ is one of the most curvilinear basic geometric shapes:It has two faces, zero vertices, and zero edges. The surface formed by the points at a fixed distance from a given straight line, the axis of the _____. The solid enclosed by this surface and by two planes perpendicular to the axis is also called a _____.

   a. BDDC
   b. 15 theorem
   c. Right circular cylinder
   d. Cylinder

4. In the various subfields of physics, there exist two common usages of the term _____, both with rigorous mathematical frameworks.

- In the study of transport phenomena (heat transfer, mass transfer and fluid dynamics), _____ is defined as the amount that flows through a unit area per unit time. _____ in this definition is a vector.
- In the field of electromagnetism and mathematics, _____ is usually the integral of a vector quantity over a finite surface. The result of this integration is a scalar quantity. The magnetic _____ is thus the integral of the magnetic vector field B over a surface, and the electric _____ is defined similarly. Using this definition, the _____ of the Poynting vector over a specified surface is the rate at which electromagnetic energy flows through that surface. Confusingly, the Poynting vector is sometimes called the power _____, which is an example of the first usage of _____, above. It has units of watts per square metre (WÂ·m^{-2})

One could argue, based on the work of James Clerk Maxwell, that the transport definition precedes the more recent way the term is used in electromagnetism. The specific quote from Maxwell is 'In the case of fluxes, we have to take the integral, over a surface, of the _____ through every element of the surface. The result of this operation is called the surface integral of the _____.

   a. Flux
   b. BIBO stability
   c. 15 theorem
   d. BDDC

5. In elementary mathematics, physics, and engineering, a _____ is a geometric object that has both a magnitude (or length), direction and sense, (i.e., orientation along the given direction.) A _____ is frequently represented by a line segment with a definite direction, or graphically as an arrow, connecting an initial point A with a terminal point B, and denoted by

The magnitude of the _____ is the length of the segment and the direction characterizes the displacement of B relative to A: how much one should move the point A to 'carry' it to the point B.

Many algebraic operations on real numbers have close analogues for vectors.

- a. Linear partial differential operator
- b. 15 theorem
- c. BDDC
- d. Vector

6. In mathematics a _____ is a construction in vector calculus which associates a vector to every point in a (locally) Euclidean space.

Vector fields are often used in physics to model, for example, the speed and direction of a moving fluid throughout space, or the strength and direction of some force, such as the magnetic or gravitational force, as it changes from point to point.

In the rigorous mathematical treatment, (tangent) vector fields are defined on manifolds as sections of a manifold's tangent bundle.

- a. BIBO stability
- b. Vector field
- c. 15 theorem
- d. BDDC

7. In mathematics, in the field of differential equations, an initial value problem is an ordinary differential equation together with specified value, called the _____, of the unknown function at a given point in the domain of the solution. In physics or other sciences, modeling a system frequently amounts to solving an initial value problem; in this context, the differential equation is an evolution equation specifying how, given initial conditions, the system will evolve with time.

An initial value problem is a differential equation

$$y'(t) = f(t, y(t)) \quad \text{with} \quad f : \mathbb{R} \times \mathbb{R} \to \mathbb{R}$$

together with a point in the domain of f

$$(t_0, y_0) \in \mathbb{R} \times \mathbb{R},$$

called the _____.

- a. Initial condition
- b. ALGOR
- c. AUSM
- d. ACTRAN

Chapter 6. APPLICATIONS OF THE INTEGRAL

8. In mathematics, in the field of differential equations, an _____ is an ordinary differential equation together with specified value, called the initial condition, of the unknown function at a given point in the domain of the solution. In physics or other sciences, modeling a system frequently amounts to solving an _____; in this context, the differential equation is an evolution equation specifying how, given initial conditions, the system will evolve with time.

An _____ is a differential equation

$$y'(t) = f(t, y(t)) \quad \text{with} \quad f : \mathbb{R} \times \mathbb{R} \to \mathbb{R}$$

together with a point in the domain of f

$$(t_0, y_0) \in \mathbb{R} \times \mathbb{R},$$

called the initial condition.

a. ALGOR
b. Initial value problem
c. ACTRAN
d. AUSM

9. In mathematics, the hyperbolic functions are analogs of the ordinary trigonometric functions. The basic hyperbolic functions are the hyperbolic sine 'sinh', and the _____ 'cosh', from which are derived the hyperbolic tangent 'tanh', etc., in analogy to the derived trigonometric functions. The inverse hyperbolic functions are the area hyperbolic sine 'arsinh' (also called 'asinh', or sometimes by the misnomer of 'arcsinh') and so on.

a. Hyperbolic cosine
b. Hyperbolic tangent
c. Square root function
d. Step function

10. In mathematics, a _____ or rhodonea curve is a sinusoid plotted in polar coordinates. Up to similarity, these curves can all be expressed by a polar equation of the form

$$r = \cos(k\theta).$$

If k is an integer, the curve will be _____ shaped with

- 2k petals if k is even, and
- k petals if k is odd.

When k is even, the entire graph of the _____ will be traced out exactly once when the value of θ changes from 0 to 2π. When k is odd, this will happen on the interval between 0 and π. (More generally, this will happen on any interval of length 2π for k even, and π for k odd.)

a. Curtate cycloid
b. Cochleoid
c. Space curve
d. Rose

11. In mathematics, engineering, and manufacturing, a _____ is a solid figure obtained by rotating a plane curve around some straight line (the axis) that lies on the same plane.

Chapter 6. APPLICATIONS OF THE INTEGRAL

Assuming that the curve does not cross the axis, the solid's volume is equal to the length of the circle described by the figure's centroid, times the figure's area (Pappus's second centroid Theorem.)

Rotating a curve

A representative disk is a three-dimensional volume element of a _____.

a. Solid of revolution
b. Riemann sum
c. Surface of revolution
d. Trigonometric substitution

12. A _____ is a special kind of space curve, i.e. a smooth curve in three-space. As a mental image of a _____ one may take the spring (although the spring is not a curve, and so is technically not a _____, it does give a convenient mental picture.) A _____ is characterised by the fact that the tangent line at any point makes a constant angle with a fixed line.
a. 15 theorem
b. BDDC
c. BIBO stability
d. Helix

13. A _____ is perfectly round geometrical object in three-dimensional space, such as the shape of a round ball. Like a circle in two dimensions, a perfect _____ is completely symmetrical around its center, with all points on the surface lying the same distance r from the center point. This distance r is known as the radius of the _____.
a. Tangent line
b. Sphere
c. North pole
d. Minimal surface

14. In mathematics, the _____ (or replacement set) of a given function is the set of 'input' values for which the function is defined. For instance, the _____ of cosine would be all real numbers, while the _____ of the square root would be only numbers greater than or equal to 0 (ignoring complex numbers in both cases.) In a representation of a function in a xy Cartesian coordinate system, the _____ is represented on the x axis (or abscissa.)
a. BDDC
b. Domain
c. BIBO stability
d. 15 theorem

15. _____ is the long dimension of any object. The _____ of a thing is the distance between its ends, its linear extent as measured from end to end. This may be distinguished from height, which is vertical extent, and width or breadth, which are the distance from side to side, measuring across the object at right angles to the _____.
a. BIBO stability
b. BDDC
c. 15 theorem
d. Length

16. Determining the _____ segment -- also called rectification of a curve -- was historically difficult. Although many methods were used for specific curves, the advent of calculus led to a general formula that provides closed-form solutions in some cases.

A curve in, say, the plane can be approximated by connecting a finite number of points on the curve using line segments to create a polygonal path. Since it is straightforward to calculate the length of each linear segment (using the theorem of Pythagoras in Euclidean space, for example), the total length of the approximation can be found by summing the lengths of each linear segment.

Chapter 6. APPLICATIONS OF THE INTEGRAL

a. Disk integration
c. Length of an irregular arc
b. Linearity of integration
d. Surface of revolution

17. Smooth functions with given closed support are used in the construction of smooth partitions of unity ; these are essential in the study of smooth manifolds, for example to show that Riemannian metrics can be defined globally starting from their local existence. A simple case is that of a bump function on the real line, that is, a _____ f that takes the value 0 outside an interval [a,b] and such that

f(x) > 0 for a < x < b.

Given a number of overlapping intervals on the line, bump functions can be constructed on each of them, and on semi-infinite intervals (->∞, c] and [d,+>∞) to cover the whole line, such that the sum of the functions is always 1.

a. Gradient
c. Continuously differentiable
b. Symmetric derivative
d. Smooth function

18. In mathematics, a (topological) _____ is defined as follows: let I be an interval of real numbers (i.e. a non-empty connected subset of $\mathbb{R}$); then a _____ γ is a continuous mapping $\gamma : I \to X$, where X is a topological space. The _____ γ is said to be simple if it is injective, i.e. if for all x, y in I, we have $\gamma(x) = \gamma(y) \implies x = y$. If I is a closed bounded interval $[a, b]$, we also allow the possibility $\gamma(a) = \gamma(b)$ (this convention makes it possible to talk about closed simple _____.)

a. Tractrix
c. Prolate cycloid
b. Curve
d. Closed curve

19. In acoustics and telecommunication, a _____ of a wave is a component frequency of the signal that is an integer multiple of the fundamental frequency. For example, if the fundamental frequency is f, the harmonics have frequencies f, 2f, 3f, 4f, etc. The harmonics have the property that they are all periodic at the fundamental frequency, therefore the sum of harmonics is also periodic at that frequency.

a. 15 theorem
c. BIBO stability
b. BDDC
d. Harmonic

20. In mathematics, the _____ is the infinite series

$$\sum_{k=1}^{\infty} \frac{1}{k} = 1 + \frac{1}{2} + \frac{1}{3} + \frac{1}{4} + \cdots.$$

Its name derives from the concept of overtones, or harmonics, in music: the wavelengths of the overtones of a vibrating string are 1/2, 1/3, 1/4, etc., of the string's fundamental wavelength. Every term of the series after the first is the harmonic mean of the neighboring terms; the term harmonic mean likewise derives from music.

The _____ diverges to infinity, albeit rather slowly (the first 10^{43} terms sum to less than 100 .)

a. BDDC
b. 15 theorem
c. Harmonic series
d. BIBO stability

21. In mathematics, the _____ is used to determine each point uniquely in a plane through two numbers, usually called the x-coordinate or abscissa and the y-coordinate or ordinate of the point. To define the coordinates, two perpendicular directed lines, are specified, as well as the unit length, which is marked off on the two axes Cartesian coordinate systems are also used in space and in higher dimensions.

a. Cylindrical coordinate system
b. Cartesian coordinate system
c. 15 theorem
d. Coordinate

22. A _____ is a surface created by rotating a curve lying on some plane (the generatrix) around a straight line (the axis of rotation) that lies on the same plane.

Examples of surfaces generated by a straight line are the cylindrical and conical surfaces. A circle that is rotated about a (coplanar) axis through the center generates a sphere.

a. Constant of integration
b. Shell integration
c. Surface of revolution
d. Riemann sum

23. A _____ is the portion of a solid--normally a cone or pyramid--which lies between two parallel planes cutting the solid. The term is commonly used in computer graphics to describe the 3d area which is visible on the screen (which is formed by a clipped pyramid.)

Each plane section is a base of the _____.

a. Frustum
b. BIBO stability
c. 15 theorem
d. BDDC

24. _____ is how much exposed area an object has. It is expressed in square units. If an object has flat faces, its _____ can be calculated by adding together the areas of its faces.

a. Lipschitz domain
b. Plane curve
c. Surface area
d. Vector area

25. The most commonly encountered form of Hooke's law is probably the spring equation, which relates the force exerted by a spring to the distance it is stretched by a _____, k, measured in force per length.

$$F = -kx$$

The negative sign indicates that the force exerted by the spring is in direct opposition to the direction of displacement. It is called a 'restoring force', as it tends to restore the system to equilibrium.

a. Polar moment of inertia
b. Spring equation
c. Spring constant
d. Navier-Stokes equations

Chapter 6. APPLICATIONS OF THE INTEGRAL

26. _____ is a type of motion in which the velocity of an object changes equal amounts in equal time periods. An example of an object having _____ would be a ball rolling down a ramp. The object picks up velocity as it goes down the ramp with equal changes in time.
  a. ACTRAN
  b. ALGOR
  c. AUSM
  d. Uniform Acceleration

27. The _____ of a system of particles is a specific point at which, for many purposes, the system's mass behaves as if it were concentrated. The _____ is a function only of the positions and masses of the particles that comprise the system. In the case of a rigid body, the position of its _____ is fixed in relation to the object (but not necessarily in contact with it.)
  a. Center of mass
  b. Fundamental lemma in the calculus of variations
  c. Simple harmonic motion
  d. 15 theorem

28. The concept of _____ in mathematics evolved from the concept of _____ in physics. The nth _____ of a real-valued function f(x) of a real variable about a value c is

$$\mu'_n = \int_{-\infty}^{\infty} (x-c)^n f(x)\, dx.$$

It is possible to define moments for random variables in a more general fashion than moments for real values. See Moments in metric spaces.

  a. Geometric mean
  b. Median
  c. Poisson distribution
  d. Moment

29. In infinitesimal calculus, a _____ is traditionally an infinitesimally small change in a variable. For example, if x is a variable, then a change in the value of x is often denoted Δx (or δx when this change is considered to be small.) The _____ dx represents such a change, but is infinitely small.
  a. Dirichlet integral
  b. Local maximum
  c. Differential
  d. The Method of Mechanical Theorems

30. In geometry, the _____, geometric center, or barycenter of a plane figure X is the intersection of all straight lines that divide X into two parts of equal moment about the line. Informally, it is the 'average' of all points of X. The definition extends to any object X in n-dimensional space: its _____ is the intersection of all hyperplanes that divide X into two parts of equal moment.
  a. BDDC
  b. 15 theorem
  c. BIBO stability
  d. Centroid

31. _____ generally conveys two primary meanings. The first is an imprecise sense of harmonious or aesthetically-pleasing proportionality and balance; such that it reflects beauty or perfection. The second meaning is a precise and well-defined concept of balance or 'patterned self-similarity' that can be demonstrated or proved according to the rules of a formal system: by geometry, through physics or otherwise.
  a. BIBO stability
  b. BDDC
  c. 15 theorem
  d. Symmetry

Chapter 6. APPLICATIONS OF THE INTEGRAL

32. In geometry, a _____ (pl. tori) is a surface of revolution generated by revolving a circle in three dimensional space about an axis coplanar with the circle, which does not touch the circle. Examples of tori include the surfaces of doughnuts and inner tubes.
    a. Prolate
    b. Hyperbolic paraboloid
    c. Paraboloid
    d. Torus

33. The _____, formerly known as the hyperbolic logarithm, is the logarithm to the base e, where e is an irrational constant approximately equal to 2.718281828. It is also sometimes referred to as the Napierian logarithm, although the original meaning of this term is slightly different. In simple terms, the _____ of a number x is the power to which e would have to be raised to equal x -- for example the natural log of e itself is 1 because e^1 = e, while the _____ of 1 would be 0, since e^0 = 1.
    a. BIBO stability
    b. Natural logarithm
    c. 15 theorem
    d. BDDC

34. The function $\log_b(x)$ depends on both b and x, but the term _____ in standard usage refers to a function of the form $\log_b(x)$ in which the base b is fixed and so the only argument is x. Thus there is one _____ for each value of the base b (which must be positive and must differ from 1.) Viewed in this way, the base-b _____ is the inverse function of the exponential function b^x.
    a. BIBO stability
    b. BDDC
    c. 15 theorem
    d. Logarithm function

35. The _____ is a function in mathematics. The application of this function to a value x is written as exp(x). Equivalently, this can be written in the form e^x, where e is a mathematical constant, the base of the natural logarithm, which equals approximately 2.718281828, and is also known as Euler's number.
    a. Exponential function
    b. Area hyperbolic functions
    c. ACTRAN
    d. Integral part

36. Just as the definite integral of a positive function of one variable represents the area of the region between the graph of the function and the x-axis, the _____ of a positive function of two variables represents the volume of the region between the surface defined by the function (on the three dimensional Cartesian plane where z = f(x,y)) and the plane which contains its domain. (Note that the same volume can be obtained via the triple integral -- the integral of a function in three variables -- of the constant function f(x, y, z) = 1 over the above-mentioned region between the surface and the plane.) If there are more variables, a multiple integral will yield hypervolumes of multi-dimensional functions.
    a. Constant of integration
    b. Trigonometric substitution
    c. Double integral
    d. Risch algorithm

37. Integration is an important concept in mathematics, specifically in the field of calculus and, more broadly, mathematical analysis. Given a function f of a real variable x and an interval [a, b] of the real line, the _____

$$\int_a^b f(x)\, dx,$$

is defined informally to be the net signed area of the region in the xy-plane bounded by the graph of f, the x-axis, and the vertical lines x = a and x = b.

Chapter 6. APPLICATIONS OF THE INTEGRAL 69

The term '_____' may also refer to the notion of antiderivative, a function F whose derivative is the given function f.

a. Integral test for convergence
b. Integral
c. Integrand
d. Indefinite integral

38. A _____ officer is an officer of high military rank. The term or equivalent is used by nearly every country in the world. _____ can be used as a generic term for all grades of _____ officer, or it can specifically refer to a single rank that is just called _____.
a. 15 theorem
b. BIBO stability
c. BDDC
d. General

39. In mathematics, the _____ are analogs of the ordinary trigonometric or circular functions. The basic _____ are the hyperbolic sine 'sinh', and the hyperbolic cosine 'cosh', from which are derived the hyperbolic tangent 'tanh', etc., in analogy to the derived trigonometric functions. The inverse _____ are the area hyperbolic sine 'arsinh' (also called 'asinh', or sometimes by the misnomer of 'arcsinh') and so on.
a. Hyperbolic cosine
b. Hyperbolic functions
c. Signum function
d. Multiplicative inverse

40. In mathematics, a _____ differential equation may refer to one of two related things, both of which are differential equations that can be attacked by a method of separation of variables.

- For ordinary differential equations, it describes a class of equations that can be separated into a pair of integrals. See: Examples of differential equations

- For partial differential equations, it describes a class of equations that can be broken down into differential equations in fewer independent variables. See _____ partial differential equation.

a. Separable
b. Method of undetermined coefficients
c. Differential equation
d. Lax pair

41. A _____ is the location at which two or more bones make contact. They are constructed to allow movement and provide mechanical support, and are classified structurally and functionally. Depiction of an intervertebral disk, a cartilaginous _____. Diagram of a synovial (diarthrosis) _____.

Joints are mainly classified structurally and functionally.

a. Joint
b. BDDC
c. BIBO stability
d. 15 theorem

42. In mathematics, the _____ of a function y = f(x) is a function that, in some fashion, 'undoes' the effect of f The _____ of f is denoted f^{-1}. The statements y=f(x) and x=f^{-1}(y) are equivalent.

a. ALGOR
b. AUSM
c. ACTRAN
d. Inverse

43. In mathematics, if f is a function from A to B then an _____ for f is a function in the opposite direction, from B to A, with the property that a round trip (a composition) from A to B to A (or from B to A to B) returns each element of the initial set to itself. Thus, if an input x into the function f produces an output y, then inputting y into the _____ f^{-1} (read f inverse, not to be confused with exponentiation) produces the output x. Not every function has an inverse; those that do are called invertible.

a. Augustin-Jean Fresnel
b. Augustin Louis Cauchy
c. Aristotle
d. Inverse function

44. An injective function is called an injection, and is also said to be a _____ function (not to be confused with _____ correspondence, i.e. a bijective function.)

A function f that is not injective is sometimes called many-to-one. (However, this terminology is also sometimes used to mean 'single-valued', i.e. each argument is mapped to at most one value.)

a. Injective function
b. One-to-one function
c. Onto
d. One-to-one

45. An injective function is called an injection, and is also said to be a _____ (not to be confused with one-to-one correspondence, i.e. a bijective function.)

A function f that is not injective is sometimes called many-to-one. (However, this terminology is also sometimes used to mean 'single-valued', i.e. each argument is mapped to at most one value.)

a. Onto
b. One-to-one
c. Injective function
d. One-to-one function

46. In calculus, a branch of mathematics, the _____ is a measurement of how a function changes when its input changes. Loosely speaking, a _____ can be thought of as how much a quantity is changing at some given point. For example, the _____ of the position (or distance) of a vehicle with respect to time is the instantaneous velocity (respectively, instantaneous speed) at which the vehicle is traveling.

The process of finding a _____ is called differentiation. The fundamental theorem of calculus states that differentiation is the reverse process to integration.

a. Stationary phase approximation
b. Bounded function
c. Semi-differentiability
d. Derivative

47. In mathematics, a function f defined on some set X with real or complex values is a _____ function, if the set of its values is _____. In other words, there exists a number M>0 such that

$$|f(x)| \leq M$$

for all x in X.

Sometimes, if $f(x) \leq A$ for all x in X, then the function is said to be _____ above by A.

- a. Bounded
- b. Stationary phase approximation
- c. Differential coefficient
- d. Concave upwards

48. In mathematics, a real-valued function f defined on an interval (or on any convex subset of some vector space) is called convex, _____, concave up or convex cup, if for any two points x and y in its domain C and any t in [0,1], we have

$$f(tx + (1-t)y) \leq tf(x) + (1-t)f(y).$$

Convex function on an interval.

In other words, a function is convex if and only if its epigraph (the set of points lying on or above the graph) is a convex set.

Pictorially, a function is called 'convex' if the function lies below the straight line segment connecting two points, for any two points in the interval.

A function is called strictly convex if

$$f(tx + (1-t)y) < tf(x) + (1-t)f(y)$$

for any t in (0,1) and $x \neq y$.

A function f is said to be concave if − f is convex.

- a. Concave upwards
- b. Vertical asymptote
- c. Third derivative
- d. Mountain pass theorem

49. A _____ is a statement of the meaning of a word or phrase. The term to be defined is known as the definiendum. The words which define it are known as the definiens.
- a. BIBO stability
- b. BDDC
- c. 15 theorem
- d. Definition

50. _____ is any physical or virtual entity that is owned by an individual or jointly by a group of individuals. An owner of _____ has the right to consume, sell, rent, mortgage, transfer and exchange his or her _____. Important widely-recognized types of _____ include real _____, personal _____ (other physical possessions), and intellectual _____ (rights over artistic creations, inventions, etc.), although the latter is not always as widely recognized or enforced.
- a. BIBO stability
- b. Property
- c. 15 theorem
- d. BDDC

Chapter 6. APPLICATIONS OF THE INTEGRAL

51. In mathematics, a _____ is an ordered list of objects (or events). Like a set, it contains members (also called elements or terms), and the number of terms (possibly infinite) is called the length of the _____. Unlike a set, order matters, and the exact same elements can appear multiple times at different positions in the _____.
    a. Y-intercept
    b. 15 theorem
    c. Slope
    d. Sequence

52. In mathematics, a _____ is an integral where the function to be integrated is evaluated along a curve. Various different line integrals are in use. A specific case of an integration along a closed curve in two dimensions or the complex plane is the contour integral.
    a. Line integral
    b. Mittag-Leffler star
    c. Radius of convergence
    d. Picard theorem

Chapter 7. TECHNIQUES OF INTEGRATION

1. In mathematics, the concept of a '_____' is used to describe the behavior of a function as its argument or input either 'gets close' to some point, or as the argument becomes arbitrarily large; or the behavior of a sequence's elements as their index increases indefinitely. Limits are used in calculus and other branches of mathematical analysis to define derivatives and continuity.

   In formulas, _____ is usually abbreviated as lim

   a. Limit
   b. 15 theorem
   c. BDDC
   d. BIBO stability

2. A _____ is a statement of the meaning of a word or phrase. The term to be defined is known as the definiendum . The words which define it are known as the definiens .
   a. 15 theorem
   b. Definition
   c. BIBO stability
   d. BDDC

3. In mathematics and its applications, a _____ system is a system for assigning an n-tuple of numbers or scalars to each point in an n-dimensional space. This concept is part of the theory of manifolds. 'Scalars' in many cases means real numbers, but, depending on context, can mean complex numbers or elements of some other commutative ring.
   a. Coordinate
   b. Cylindrical coordinate system
   c. Spherical coordinate system
   d. 15 theorem

4. Integration is an important concept in mathematics, specifically in the field of calculus and, more broadly, mathematical analysis. Given a function f of a real variable x and an interval [a, b] of the real line, the _____

   $$\int_a^b f(x)\,dx,$$

   is defined informally to be the net signed area of the region in the xy-plane bounded by the graph of f, the x-axis, and the vertical lines x = a and x = b.

   The term '_____' may also refer to the notion of antiderivative, a function F whose derivative is the given function f.

   a. Integrand
   b. Indefinite integral
   c. Integral test for convergence
   d. Integral

5. The _____ of an angle is the ratio of the length of the adjacent side to the length of the hypotenuse. In our case

   $$\cos A = \frac{\text{adjacent}}{\text{hypotenuse}} = \frac{b}{h}.$$

The tangent of an angle is the ratio of the length of the opposite side to the length of the adjacent side. In our case

$$\tan A = \frac{\text{opposite}}{\text{adjacent}} = \frac{a}{b}.$$

The remaining three functions are best defined using the above three functions.

    a. Trigonometric   b. Sine integral
    c. Trigonometric functions   d. Cosine

6. The _____ of an angle is the ratio of the length of the opposite side to the length of the hypotenuse. In our case

$$\sin A = \frac{\text{opposite}}{\text{hypotenuse}} = \frac{a}{h}.$$

Note that this ratio does not depend on size of the particular right triangle chosen, as long as it contains the angle A, since all such triangles are similar.

The cosine of an angle is the ratio of the length of the adjacent side to the length of the hypotenuse.

    a. Trigonometric   b. Sine integral
    c. Trigonometric functions   d. Sine

7. In integral calculus we would want to write a fractional algebraic expression as the sum of its _____ in order to take the integral of each simple fraction separately. Once the original denominator, D_0, has been factored we set up a fraction for each factor in the denominator. We may use a subscripted D to represent the denominator of the respective _____ which are the factors in D_0.

    a. Left inverse   b. Closed-form expression
    c. Multinomial theorem   d. Partial fractions

8. In mathematics, a _____ or quadratic is a polynomial of degree two. A _____ may involve a single variable x, or multiple variables such as x, y, and z.

Any single-variable _____ may be written as

$$ax^2 + bx + c,$$

where x is the variable, and a, b, and c represent the coefficients.

    a. Characteristic equation   b. Difference polynomial
    c. Binomial type   d. Quadratic polynomial

Chapter 7. TECHNIQUES OF INTEGRATION

9. In mathematics, a _____ is any function which can be written as the ratio of two polynomial functions.

$$y = \frac{x^2 - 3x - 2}{x^2 - 4}$$

In the case of one variable, x, a _____ is a function of the form

$$f(x) = \frac{P(x)}{Q(x)}$$

where P and Q are polynomial function in x and Q is not the zero polynomial. The domain of f is the set of all points x for which the denominator Q(x) is not zero.

a. Rational function
b. BIBO stability
c. 15 theorem
d. BDDC

10. Trigonometry is a branch of mathematics that deals with triangles, particularly those plane triangles in which one angle has 90 degrees (right triangles.) Trigonometry deals with relationships between the sides and the angles of triangles and with the _____ functions, which describe those relationships.

Trigonometry has applications in both pure mathematics and in applied mathematics, where it is essential in many branches of science and technology.

a. Sine
b. Trigonometric integrals
c. Trigonometric
d. Trigonometric functions

11. In mathematics, _____ is the substitution of trigonometric functions for other expressions. One may use the trigonometric identities to simplify certain integrals containing radical expressions:

- If the integrand contains

$$\sqrt{a^2 - x^2},$$

let

$$x = a \sin \theta$$

and use the identity

$$1 - \sin^2\theta = \cos^2\theta.$$

- If the integrand contains
$$\sqrt{a^2 + x^2}$$
let $x = a\tan\theta$ and use the identity
$$1 + \tan^2\theta = \sec^2\theta.$$

- If the integrand contains
$$\sqrt{x^2 - a^2}$$
let
$$x = a\sec\theta$$
and use the identity
$$\sec^2\theta - 1 = \tan^2\theta.$$

In the integral
$$\int \frac{dx}{\sqrt{a^2 - x^2}}$$

we may use
$$x = a\sin(\theta),\ dx = a\cos(\theta)\,d\theta$$
$$\theta = \arcsin\left(\frac{x}{a}\right)$$

so that the integral becomes
$$\int \frac{dx}{\sqrt{a^2 - x^2}} = \int \frac{a\cos(\theta)\,d\theta}{\sqrt{a^2 - a^2\sin^2(\theta)}} = \int \frac{a\cos(\theta)\,d\theta}{\sqrt{a^2(1 - \sin^2(\theta))}}$$
$$= \int \frac{a\cos(\theta)\,d\theta}{\sqrt{a^2\cos^2(\theta)}} = \int d\theta = \theta + C = \arcsin\left(\frac{x}{a}\right) + C$$

Note that the above step requires that a > 0 and cos(θ) > 0; we can choose the a to be the positive square root of a^2; and we impose the restriction on θ to be −π/2 < θ < π/2 by using the arcsin function.

For a definite integral, one must figure out how the bounds of integration change. For example, as x goes from 0 to a/2, then sin (θ) goes from 0 to 1/2, so θ goes from 0 to π/6.

- a. Surface of revolution
- b. Rectangle method
- c. Riemann sum
- d. Trigonometric substitution

12. In geometry, a _____ (pl. tori) is a surface of revolution generated by revolving a circle in three dimensional space about an axis coplanar with the circle, which does not touch the circle. Examples of tori include the surfaces of doughnuts and inner tubes.
- a. Prolate
- b. Hyperbolic paraboloid
- c. Paraboloid
- d. Torus

13. In mathematics, a _____ is a definite integral taken over a surface (which may be a curved set in space); it can be thought of as the double integral analog of the line integral. Given a surface, one may integrate over it scalar fields (that is, functions which return numbers as values), and vector fields (that is, functions which return vectors as values.)

Surface integrals have applications in physics, particularly with the classical theory of electromagnetism.

- a. Contact
- b. Surface integral
- c. Differential operator
- d. Symmetry of second derivatives

14. The _____ is an important partial differential equation which describes the distribution of heat (or variation in temperature) in a given region over time. For a function u(x,y,z,t) of three spatial variables (x,y,z) and the time variable t, the _____ is

$$\frac{\partial u}{\partial t} - k\left(\frac{\partial^2 u}{\partial x^2} + \frac{\partial^2 u}{\partial y^2} + \frac{\partial^2 u}{\partial z^2}\right) = 0$$

or equivalently

$$\frac{\partial u}{\partial t} = k\nabla^2 u$$

where k is a constant.

The _____ is of fundamental importance in diverse scientific fields.

- a. BIBO stability
- b. Heat equation
- c. 15 theorem
- d. BDDC

15. In calculus, an _____ is the limit of a definite integral as an endpoint of the interval of integration approaches either a specified real number or ∞ or −∞ or, in some cases, as both endpoints approach limits.

Specifically, an _____ is a limit of the form

$$\lim_{b\to\infty} \int_a^b f(x)\,dx, \qquad \lim_{a\to -\infty} \int_a^b f(x)\,dx,$$

or of the form

$$\lim_{c\to b^-} \int_a^c f(x)\,dx, \qquad \lim_{c\to a^+} \int_c^b f(x)\,dx,$$

in which one takes a limit in one or the other (or sometimes both) endpoints. Improper integrals may also occur at an interior point of the domain of integration, or at multiple such points.

    a. Improper integral   b. ALGOR
    c. AUSM   d. ACTRAN

16. A _____ officer is an officer of high military rank. The term or equivalent is used by nearly every country in the world. _____ can be used as a generic term for all grades of _____ officer, or it can specifically refer to a single rank that is just called _____.
    a. BDDC   b. 15 theorem
    c. BIBO stability   d. General

17. In mathematics, a _____ to an ordinary or partial differential equation is a function for which the derivatives appearing in the equation may not all exist but which is nonetheless deemed to satisfy the equation in some precisely defined sense. There are many different definitions of _____, appropriate for different classes of equations. One of the most important is based on the notion of distributions.
    a. Structural stability   b. Singular perturbation
    c. Weak solution   d. Conserved quantity

18. In physics, _____ is the speed where the kinetic energy of an object is equal to the magnitude of its gravitational potential energy, as calculated by the equation,

$$U_g = \frac{-Gm_1 m_2}{r}.$$

It is commonly described as the speed needed to 'break free' from a gravitational field (without any additional impulse.) The term _____ can be considered a misnomer because it is actually a speed rather than a velocity, i.e. it specifies how fast the object must move but the direction of movement is irrelevant, unless 'downward.' In more technical terms, _____ is a scalar (and not a vector.)

The phenomenon of _____ is a consequence of conservation of energy.

Chapter 7. TECHNIQUES OF INTEGRATION

    a. AUSM
    c. ALGOR
    b. ACTRAN
    d. Escape velocity

19. In physics, _____ is defined as the rate of change of position. it is vector physical quantity; both speed and direction are required to define it. In the SI (metric) system, it is measured in meters per second: (m/s) or ms^{-1}.

    a. BIBO stability
    c. BDDC
    b. 15 theorem
    d. Velocity

20. _____ is a way of expressing knowledge or belief that an event will occur or has occurred. In mathematics the concept has been given an exact meaning in _____ theory, that is used extensively in such areas of study as mathematics, statistics, finance, gambling, science, and philosophy to draw conclusions about the likelihood of potential events and the underlying mechanics of complex systems.

The word _____ does not have a consistent direct definition.

    a. Normal distribution
    c. Linear regression
    b. Discrete probability distributions
    d. Probability

21. In statistics, _____ is a simple measure of the variability or dispersion of a data set. A low _____ indicates that all of the data points are very close to the same value (the mean), while high _____ indicates that the data is 'spread out' over a large range of values.

For example, the average height for adult men in the United States is about 70 inches, with a _____ of around 3 inches.

    a. Correlation
    c. Poisson distribution
    b. Standard deviation
    d. Continuous random variable

22. In probability theory and statistics, the _____ (or expectation value or mean and for continuous random variables with a density function it is the probability density -weighted integral of the possible values.

The term '_____' can be misleading.

    a. Expected value
    c. ACTRAN
    b. ALGOR
    d. AUSM

Chapter 8. DIFFERENTIAL EQUATIONS

1. In physics and geometry, the _____ is the theoretical shape of a hanging flexible chain or cable when supported at its ends and acted upon by a uniform gravitational force (its own weight) and in equilibrium. The curve has a U shape that is similar in appearance to the parabola, though it is a different curve.
   a. BIBO stability
   b. BDDC
   c. 15 theorem
   d. Catenary

2. In mathematics, even functions and odd functions are functions which satisfy particular symmetry relations, with respect to taking additive inverses. They are important in many areas of mathematical analysis, especially the theory of power series and Fourier series. They are named for the parity of the powers of the power functions which satisfy each condition: the function $f(x) = x^n$ is an _____ if n is an even integer, and it is an odd function if n is an odd integer.
   a. Integral of secant cubed
   b. Infinite series
   c. Even function
   d. Operational calculus

3. In mathematics and its applications, a _____ system is a system for assigning an n-tuple of numbers or scalars to each point in an n-dimensional space. This concept is part of the theory of manifolds. 'Scalars' in many cases means real numbers, but, depending on context, can mean complex numbers or elements of some other commutative ring.
   a. Cylindrical coordinate system
   b. Spherical coordinate system
   c. 15 theorem
   d. Coordinate

4. In mathematics, a _____ (or critical number) is a point on the domain of a function where:

   - one dimension: the derivative (or slope of the line when visualized) is equal to zero or a point where the function ceases to be differentiable.
   - in general: there are two distinct concepts: either the derivative (Jacobian) vanishes, or it is not of full rank (or, in either case, the function is not differentiable); these agree in one dimension.

   Note that in one dimension, a critical value or critical number x of function f is the domain element at which the derivative is zero or undefined, whereas the associated ordered pair (x, y) is the _____. In higher dimensions a critical value is in the range whereas a _____ is in the domain.

   There are two situations in which a point becomes a _____ of a function of one variable. The first of which is that the value of the first derivative is equal to zero.

   a. Critical point
   b. Multivariable calculus
   c. Total derivative
   d. Differentiation operator

5. A _____ officer is an officer of high military rank. The term or equivalent is used by nearly every country in the world. _____ can be used as a generic term for all grades of _____ officer, or it can specifically refer to a single rank that is just called _____.
   a. BIBO stability
   b. 15 theorem
   c. BDDC
   d. General

6. In mathematics, a _____ to an ordinary or partial differential equation is a function for which the derivatives appearing in the equation may not all exist but which is nonetheless deemed to satisfy the equation in some precisely defined sense. There are many different definitions of _____, appropriate for different classes of equations. One of the most important is based on the notion of distributions.

a. Singular perturbation
c. Weak solution

b. Conserved quantity
d. Structural stability

7. In mathematics, the _____ are analogs of the ordinary trigonometric or circular functions. The basic _____ are the hyperbolic sine 'sinh', and the hyperbolic cosine 'cosh', from which are derived the hyperbolic tangent 'tanh', etc., in analogy to the derived trigonometric functions. The inverse _____ are the area hyperbolic sine 'arsinh' (also called 'asinh', or sometimes by the misnomer of 'arcsinh') and so on.

a. Multiplicative inverse
c. Hyperbolic cosine

b. Hyperbolic functions
d. Signum function

8. In mathematics, in the field of differential equations, an initial value problem is an ordinary differential equation together with specified value, called the _____, of the unknown function at a given point in the domain of the solution. In physics or other sciences, modeling a system frequently amounts to solving an initial value problem; in this context, the differential equation is an evolution equation specifying how, given initial conditions, the system will evolve with time.

An initial value problem is a differential equation

$$y'(t) = f(t, y(t)) \quad \text{with} \quad f : \mathbb{R} \times \mathbb{R} \to \mathbb{R}$$

together with a point in the domain of f

$$(t_0, y_0) \in \mathbb{R} \times \mathbb{R},$$

called the _____.

a. ALGOR
c. AUSM

b. ACTRAN
d. Initial condition

9. _____ is the change in population over time, and can be quantified as the change in the number of individuals in a population using 'per unit time' for measurement. The term _____ can technically refer to any species, but almost always refers to humans, and it is often used informally for the more specific demographic term _____ rate, and is often used to refer specifically to the growth of the population of the world.

Simple models of _____ include the Malthusian Growth Model and the logistic model.

a. BDDC
c. 15 theorem

b. BIBO stability
d. Population growth

10. In mathematics, an _____ is a generalization for the concept of a function in which the dependent variable has not been given 'explicitly' in terms of the independent variable. To give a function f explicitly is to provide a prescription for determining the output value of the function y in terms of the input value x:

y = f(x.)

By contrast, the function is implicit if the value of y is obtained from x by solving an equation of the form:

R(x,y) = 0.

a. Implicit function
b. Implicit differentiation
c. Ordinary differential equation
d. Automatic differentiation

11. In the branch of mathematics called multivariable calculus, the _____ is a tool which allows relations to be converted to functions. It does this by representing the relation as the graph of a function. There may not be a single function whose graph is the entire relation, but there may be such a function on a restriction of the domain of the relation.
    a. Upper convected time derivative
    b. Isoperimetric inequality
    c. Implicit function theorem
    d. Inverse function theorem

12. In calculus, an _____, primitive or indefinite integral of a function f is a function F whose derivative is equal to f, i.e., F >' = f. The process of solving for antiderivatives is antidifferentiation (or indefinite integration.) Antiderivatives are related to definite integrals through the fundamental theorem of calculus: the definite integral of a function over an interval is equal to the difference between the values of an _____ evaluated at the endpoints of the interval.
    a. Order of integration
    b. Indefinite integral
    c. Integrand
    d. Antiderivative

13. In infinitesimal calculus, a _____ is traditionally an infinitesimally small change in a variable. For example, if x is a variable, then a change in the value of x is often denoted Δx (or δx when this change is considered to be small.) The _____ dx represents such a change, but is infinitely small.
    a. The Method of Mechanical Theorems
    b. Differential
    c. Dirichlet integral
    d. Local maximum

14. A _____ is a model used within physics to explain how gravity exists in the universe. In its original concept, gravity was a force between point masses. Following Newton, Laplace attempted to model gravity as some kind of radiation field or fluid, and since the 19th century explanations for gravity have usually been sought in terms of a field model, rather than a point attraction.
    a. BDDC
    b. Gravitational field
    c. BIBO stability
    d. 15 theorem

15. Integration is an important concept in mathematics, specifically in the field of calculus and, more broadly, mathematical analysis. Given a function f of a real variable x and an interval [a, b] of the real line, the _____

$$\int_a^b f(x)\,dx,$$

is defined informally to be the net signed area of the region in the xy-plane bounded by the graph of f, the x-axis, and the vertical lines x = a and x = b.

The term '_____' may also refer to the notion of antiderivative, a function F whose derivative is the given function f.

a. Integrand
b. Integral test for convergence
c. Indefinite integral
d. Integral

16. In mathematics, a (topological) _____ is defined as follows: let I be an interval of real numbers (i.e. a non-empty connected subset of $\mathbb{R}$); then a _____ γ is a continuous mapping $\gamma : I \to X$, where X is a topological space. The _____ γ is said to be simple if it is injective, i.e. if for all x, y in I, we have $\gamma(x) = \gamma(y) \implies x = y$. If I is a closed bounded interval $[a, b]$, we also allow the possibility $\gamma(a) = \gamma(b)$ (this convention makes it possible to talk about closed simple _____.)

a. Curve
b. Prolate cycloid
c. Tractrix
d. Closed curve

17. A _____ is a mathematical equation for an unknown function of one or several variables that relates the values of the function itself and of its derivatives of various orders. they play a prominent role in engineering, physics, economics and other disciplines.

A simplified real world example of a _____ is modeling the acceleration of a ball falling through the air (considering only gravity and air resistance.)

a. Phase line
b. Caloric polynomial
c. Structural stability
d. Differential equation

18. _____ (including exponential decay) occurs when the growth rate of a mathematical function is proportional to the function's current value. In the case of a discrete domain of definition with equal intervals it is also called geometric growth or geometric decay (the function values form a geometric progression.)

_____ is said to follow an exponential law; the simple-_____ model is known as the Malthusian growth model.

a. Oscillating
b. Inseparable differential equation
c. Isomonodromic deformation
d. Exponential growth

19. The _____ of a quantity whose value decreases with time is the interval required for the quantity to decay to half of its initial value. The concept originated in describing how long it takes atoms to undergo radioactive decay but also applies in a wide variety of other situations.

The term '_____' dates to 1907.

a. BDDC
b. BIBO stability
c. 15 theorem
d. Half-life

20. _____ is a type of motion in which the velocity of an object changes equal amounts in equal time periods. An example of an object having _____ would be a ball rolling down a ramp. The object picks up velocity as it goes down the ramp with equal changes in time.

a. Uniform Acceleration
b. ACTRAN
c. ALGOR
d. AUSM

21. In mathematics, a _____ (or direction field) is a graphical representation of the solutions of a first-order differential equation. It is achieved without solving the differential equation analytically, and thence it is useful. The representation may be used to qualitatively visualise solutions, or to numerically approximate them.
    a. Slope field
    b. Continuous function
    c. Visual Calculus
    d. Leibniz function

22. _____ is used to describe the steepness, incline, gradient, or grade of a straight line. A higher _____ value indicates a steeper incline. The _____ is defined as the ratio of the 'rise' divided by the 'run' between two points on a line, or in other words, the ratio of the altitude change to the horizontal distance between any two points on the line.
    a. 15 theorem
    b. Y-intercept
    c. Slope
    d. Sequence

23. The _____ of a biological species in an environment is the population size of the species that the environment can sustain in the long term, given the food, habitat, water and other necessities available in the environment. For the human population, more complex variables such as sanitation and medical care are sometimes considered as part of the necessary infrastructure.

As population density increases, birth rate often increases and death rate typically decreases.

    a. BDDC
    b. Carrying capacity
    c. 15 theorem
    d. BIBO stability

24. In physics, _____ is defined as the rate of change of position. it is vector physical quantity; both speed and direction are required to define it. In the SI (metric) system, it is measured in meters per second: (m/s) or ms^{-1}.
    a. 15 theorem
    b. BDDC
    c. BIBO stability
    d. Velocity

25. In mathematics, a _____ differential equation may refer to one of two related things, both of which are differential equations that can be attacked by a method of separation of variables.

- For ordinary differential equations, it describes a class of equations that can be separated into a pair of integrals. See: Examples of differential equations

- For partial differential equations, it describes a class of equations that can be broken down into differential equations in fewer independent variables. See _____ partial differential equation.

    a. Method of undetermined coefficients
    b. Lax pair
    c. Separable
    d. Differential equation

26. A _____ $y_s(x)$ of an ordinary differential equation is a solution that is tangent to every solution from the family of general solutions. By tangent we mean that there is a point x where $y_s(x) = y_c(x)$ and $y'_s(x) = y'_c(x)$ where y_c is any general solution.

Chapter 8. DIFFERENTIAL EQUATIONS

Usually, singular solutions appear in differential equations when there is a need to divide in a term that might be equal to zero.

- a. Method of undetermined coefficients
- b. Conserved quantity
- c. Method of matched asymptotic expansions
- d. Singular solution

27. In mathematics, a _____ is a differential equation of the form

$$Ly = f$$

where the differential operator L is a linear operator, y is the unknown function, and the right hand side f is a given function (called the source term.) The linearity condition on L rules out operations such as taking the square of the derivative of y; but permits, for example, taking the second derivative of y. Therefore a fairly general form of such an equation would be

$$a_n(x)D^n y(x) + a_{n-1}(x)D^{n-1}y(x) + \cdots + a_1(x)Dy(x) + a_0(x)y(x) = f(x)$$

where D is the differential operator d/dx (i.e. Dy = y' , D^2y = y',...), and the a_i are given functions.

- a. Linear differential equation
- b. Method of undetermined coefficients
- c. Stochastic differential equation
- d. Petrovsky lacuna

28. In a totally ordered set all elements are mutually comparable, so such a set can have at most one minimal element and at most one maximal element. Then, due to mutual comparability, the minimal element will also be the least element and the maximal element will also be the greatest element. Thus in a totally ordered set we can simply use the terms minimum and _____.

- a. Nth term
- b. Maximum
- c. Leibniz rule
- d. Racetrack principle

29. In a totally ordered set all elements are mutually comparable, so such a set can have at most one minimal element and at most one maximal element. Then, due to mutual comparability, the minimal element will also be the least element and the maximal element will also be the greatest element. Thus in a totally ordered set we can simply use the terms _____ and maximum.

- a. Minimum
- b. Ghosts of departed quantities
- c. Maximum
- d. Nth term

30. In geometry, the _____ (or simply the tangent) to a curve at a given point is the straight line that 'just touches' the curve at that point (in the sense explained more precisely below.) As it passes through the point of tangency, the _____ is 'going in the same direction' as the curve, and in this sense it is the best straight-line approximation to the curve at that point. The same definition applies to space curves and curves in n-dimensional Euclidean space.

- a. North pole
- b. Lie derivative
- c. Minimal surface
- d. Tangent line

31. In mathematics, an _____ is a function that is chosen to facilitate the solving of a given ordinary differential equation.

Consider an ordinary differential equation of the form

$$y' + a(x)y = b(x) \qquad (1)$$

where y = y(x) is an unknown function of x, and a(x) and b(x) are given functions.

The _____ method works by turning the left hand side into the form of the derivative of a product.

a. Exponential growth
b. Integrating factor
c. Oscillating
d. Isomonodromic deformation

32. Cantor defined two kinds of _____ numbers, the ordinal numbers and the cardinal numbers. Ordinal numbers may be identified with well-ordered sets, or counting carried on to any stopping point, including points after an _____ number have already been counted. Generalizing finite and the ordinary _____ sequences which are maps from the positive integers leads to mappings from ordinal numbers, and transfinite sequences.

a. ACTRAN
b. ALGOR
c. AUSM
d. Infinite

33. The terms of the series are often produced according to a certain rule, such as by a formula, by an algorithm, by a sequence of measurements, or even by a random number generator. As there are an infinite number of terms, this notion is often called an _____. Unlike finite summations, series need tools from mathematical analysis to be fully understood and manipulated.

a. Extreme value
b. Infinite Series
c. Extreme Value Theorem
d. Integration by substitution

34. A _____ is the location at which two or more bones make contact. They are constructed to allow movement and provide mechanical support, and are classified structurally and functionally. Depiction of an intervertebral disk, a cartilaginous _____. Diagram of a synovial (diarthrosis) _____.

Joints are mainly classified structurally and functionally.

a. 15 theorem
b. BIBO stability
c. Joint
d. BDDC

35. In mathematics, the concept of a '_____' is used to describe the behavior of a function as its argument or input either 'gets close' to some point, or as the argument becomes arbitrarily large; or the behavior of a sequence's elements as their index increases indefinitely. Limits are used in calculus and other branches of mathematical analysis to define derivatives and continuity.

In formulas, _____ is usually abbreviated as lim

Chapter 8. DIFFERENTIAL EQUATIONS

a. BIBO stability
b. BDDC
c. 15 theorem
d. Limit

36. _____ is the introduction of contaminants into an environment that causes instability, disorder, harm or discomfort to the ecosystem i.e. physical systems or living organisms. _____ can take the form of chemical substances, or energy, such as noise, heat, or light energy. Pollutants, the elements of _____, can be foreign substances or energies, or naturally occurring; when naturally occurring, they are considered contaminants when they exceed natural levels.

a. BIBO stability
b. 15 theorem
c. BDDC
d. Pollution

37. The _____ are a pair of first order, non-linear, differential equations frequently used to describe the dynamics of biological systems in which two species interact, one a predator and one its prey. They were proposed independently by Alfred J. Lotka in 1925 and Vito Volterra in 1926.

where

- y is the number of some predator;
- x is the number of its prey;
- dy/dt and dx/dt represents the growth of the two populations against time;
- t represents the time; and
- $>\alpha$, $>\beta$, $>\gamma$ and $>\delta$ are parameters representing the interaction of the two species.

When multiplied out, the equations take a form useful for physical interpretation. Their origin should be considered from a more general framework,

where both functions represent per capita growth rates of the prey and predator, respectively.

a. 15 theorem
b. BDDC
c. BIBO stability
d. Lotka-Volterra equations

38. In mathematics, _____ are a concept central to linear algebra and related fields of mathematics

Suppose that K is a field and V is a vector space over K. As usual, we call elements of V vectors and call elements of K scalars.

a. 15 theorem
b. Permutation
c. Fundamental theorem of algebra
d. Linear combinations

39. In mathematics, a _____ is a constant multiplicative factor of a certain object. For example, in the expression $9x^2$, the _____ of x^2 is 9.

The object can be such things as a variable, a vector, a function, etc.

a. Resultant
b. Degree of the polynomial
c. Binomial type
d. Coefficient

40. In mathematics, constant coefficients is a term applied to differential operators, and also some difference operators, to signify that they contain no functions of the independent variables, other than constant functions. In other words, it singles out special operators, within the larger class of operators having variable coefficients. Such _____ operators have been found to be the easiest to handle, in several respects.

a. Semi-elliptic operator
b. Constant coefficient
c. Dirac operator
d. Laplacian

41. In mathematics, a _____ is an ordered list of objects (or events). Like a set, it contains members (also called elements or terms), and the number of terms (possibly infinite) is called the length of the _____. Unlike a set, order matters, and the exact same elements can appear multiple times at different positions in the _____.

a. Y-intercept
b. 15 theorem
c. Sequence
d. Slope

42. In mathematics, an _____ is informally a function which satisfies a polynomial equation whose coefficients are themselves polynomials. For example, an _____ in one variable x is a solution y for an equation

$$a_n(x)y^n + a_{n-1}(x)y^{n-1} + \cdots + a_0(x) = 0$$

where the coefficients $a_i(x)$ are polynomial functions of x. A function which is not algebraic is called a transcendental function.

a. ACTRAN
b. ALGOR
c. AUSM
d. Algebraic function

43. In discrete mathematics, the _____ is used when solving recurrence problems. One can specify a recurrence relation of the form

$$t_n = At_{n-1} + Bt_{n-2}$$

where the value of t_n is dependent on the values of t_{n-1} and t_{n-2}. When solving a recurrence relation, the goal is to eliminate this dependency and derive an equation of the form

$$t_n = c_1 r_1^n + c_2 r_2^n,$$

where c_1 and c_2 are constants and r_1 and r_2 are the roots of the _____

$$r^2 - Ar - B = 0,$$

where A and B are the constants defined in the original recurrence relation.

- a. Sheffer sequence
- b. Characteristic equation
- c. Leading coefficient
- d. Discriminant

44. _____ is any effect, either deliberately engendered or inherent to a system, that tends to reduce the amplitude of oscillations of an oscillatory system.

In physics and engineering, _____ may be mathematically modelled as a force synchronous with the velocity of the object but opposite in direction to it. If such force is also proportional to the velocity, as for a simple mechanical viscous damper (dashpot), the force F may be related to the velocity v by

$$\mathbf{F} = -c\mathbf{v}$$

where c is the viscous _____ coefficient, given in units of newton-seconds per meter.

- a. BIBO stability
- b. BDDC
- c. 15 theorem
- d. Damping

45. The most commonly encountered form of Hooke's law is probably the spring equation, which relates the force exerted by a spring to the distance it is stretched by a _____, k, measured in force per length.

$$F = -kx$$

The negative sign indicates that the force exerted by the spring is in direct opposition to the direction of displacement. It is called a 'restoring force', as it tends to restore the system to equilibrium.

- a. Polar moment of inertia
- b. Navier-Stokes equations
- c. Spring equation
- d. Spring constant

46. In computer science and information science, _____ could also be a method or an algorithm. Again, an example will illustrate: There are systems of counting, as with Roman numerals, and various systems for filing papers, or catalogues, and various library systems, of which the Dewey Decimal _____ is an example. This still fits with the definition of components which are connected together (in this case in order to facilitate the flow of information.)

Chapter 8. DIFFERENTIAL EQUATIONS

    a. BDDC
    c. 15 theorem
    b. BIBO stability
    d. System

47. In vector calculus, the _____ is an operator that measures the magnitude of a vector field's source or sink at a given point; the _____ of a vector field is a (signed) scalar. For example, consider air as it is heated or cooled. The relevant vector field for this example is the velocity of the moving air at a point.
    a. Divergence
    c. Green's theorem
    b. Gradient theorem
    d. Triple product

48. In elementary mathematics, physics, and engineering, a _____ is a geometric object that has both a magnitude (or length), direction and sense, (i.e., orientation along the given direction.) A _____ is frequently represented by a line segment with a definite direction, or graphically as an arrow, connecting an initial point A with a terminal point B, and denoted by

$\boxed{\times}\,\vec{}$

The magnitude of the _____ is the length of the segment and the direction characterizes the displacement of B relative to A: how much one should move the point A to 'carry' it to the point B.

Many algebraic operations on real numbers have close analogues for vectors.

    a. Linear partial differential operator
    c. 15 theorem
    b. Vector
    d. BDDC

49. In mathematics a _____ is a construction in vector calculus which associates a vector to every point in a (locally) Euclidean space.

Vector fields are often used in physics to model, for example, the speed and direction of a moving fluid throughout space, or the strength and direction of some force, such as the magnetic or gravitational force, as it changes from point to point.

In the rigorous mathematical treatment, (tangent) vector fields are defined on manifolds as sections of a manifold's tangent bundle.

    a. BDDC
    c. 15 theorem
    b. BIBO stability
    d. Vector field

50. _____ is the motion of a simple harmonic oscillator, a motion that is neither driven nor damped. The motion is periodic - as it repeats itself at standard intervals in a specific manner - and sinusoidal, with constant amplitude; the acceleration of a body executing _____ is directly proportional to the displacement of the body from the equilibrium position and is always directed towards the equilibrium position.

The motion is characterized by its amplitude (which is always positive), its period, the time for a single oscillation, its frequency, the reciprocal of the period (i.e. the number of cycles per unit time), and its phase, which determines the starting point on the sine wave.

Chapter 8. DIFFERENTIAL EQUATIONS

a. Holonomic
b. 15 theorem
c. Fundamental lemma in the calculus of variations
d. Simple harmonic motion

51. In acoustics and telecommunication, a _____ of a wave is a component frequency of the signal that is an integer multiple of the fundamental frequency. For example, if the fundamental frequency is f, the harmonics have frequencies f, 2f, 3f, 4f, etc. The harmonics have the property that they are all periodic at the fundamental frequency, therefore the sum of harmonics is also periodic at that frequency.

a. Harmonic
b. BIBO stability
c. 15 theorem
d. BDDC

52. In mathematics, the hyperbolic functions are analogs of the ordinary trigonometric functions. The basic hyperbolic functions are the hyperbolic sine 'sinh', and the _____ 'cosh', from which are derived the hyperbolic tangent 'tanh', etc., in analogy to the derived trigonometric functions. The inverse hyperbolic functions are the area hyperbolic sine 'arsinh' (also called 'asinh', or sometimes by the misnomer of 'arcsinh') and so on.

a. Square root function
b. Step function
c. Hyperbolic cosine
d. Hyperbolic tangent

53. _____ is the magnitude of change in the oscillating variable, with each oscillation, within an oscillating system. For instance, sound waves are oscillations in atmospheric pressure and their amplitudes are proportional to the change in pressure during one oscillation. If the variable undergoes regular oscillations, and a graph of the system is drawn with the oscillating variable as the vertical axis and time as the horizontal axis, the _____ is visually represented by the vertical distance between the extrema of the curve.

a. AUSM
b. ALGOR
c. ACTRAN
d. Amplitude

54. In mathematics, the _____ of a function is the set of all 'output' values produced by that function. Sometimes it is called the image, or more precisely, the image of the domain of the function. If a function is a surjection then its _____ is equal to its codomain.

a. Range
b. Surjective
c. Constant function
d. Piecewise-defined function

55. In mathematics, in the field of ordinary differential equations, a non trivial solution to an ordinary differential equation

$$F(x, y, y', \ldots, y^{(n-1)}) = y^{(n)} \quad x \in [0, +\infty)$$

is called _____ if it has an infinite number of roots, otherwise it is called non-_____. The differential equation is called _____ if it has an _____ solution.

The differential equation

$$y'' + y = 0$$

is _____ as sin(x) is a solution.

a. Integrating factor
c. Exponential growth
b. Oscillating
d. Inseparable differential equation

56. _____ is how much exposed area an object has. It is expressed in square units. If an object has flat faces, its _____ can be calculated by adding together the areas of its faces.
   a. Lipschitz domain
   c. Surface area
   b. Vector area
   d. Plane curve

Chapter 9. POLAR COORDINATES AND PARAMETRIC CURVES

1. In mathematics, a _____ (or just conic) is a curve obtained by intersecting a cone (more precisely, a circular conical surface) with a plane. A _____ is therefore a restriction of a quadric surface to the plane. The conic sections were named and studied as long ago as 200 BC, when Apollonius of Perga undertook a systematic study of their properties.
   a. Latus rectum
   b. 15 theorem
   c. BDDC
   d. Conic section

2. _____ generally conveys two primary meanings. The first is an imprecise sense of harmonious or aesthetically-pleasing proportionality and balance; such that it reflects beauty or perfection. The second meaning is a precise and well-defined concept of balance or 'patterned self-similarity' that can be demonstrated or proved according to the rules of a formal system: by geometry, through physics or otherwise.
   a. 15 theorem
   b. BIBO stability
   c. BDDC
   d. Symmetry

3. In mathematics, an _____, is the apparent shape of a circle viewed obliquely from outside it, as distinct from a hyperbola which is the shape seen from inside. It is the finite or bounded case of a conic section as a shape cut in a cone by a plane, the unbounded cases being the parabola, which like the _____ remains connected, and the hyperbola, which separates into two connected components or branches.

   Equivalently an _____ can be defined as the locus of points, or path traced out, in a plane such that the sum of the distances from the moving point to two fixed points remains constant.

   a. AUSM
   b. ACTRAN
   c. ALGOR
   d. Ellipse

4. In mathematics, the _____ is a conic section, the intersection of a right circular conical surface and a plane parallel to a generating straight line of that surface. Given a point (the focus) and a line (the directrix) that lie in a plane, the locus of points in that plane that are equidistant to them is a _____.

   A particular case arises when the plane is tangent to the conical surface of a circle.

   a. BIBO stability
   b. Parabola
   c. BDDC
   d. 15 theorem

5. The terms '_____' and 'independent variable' are used in similar but subtly different ways in mathematics and statistics as part of the standard terminology in those subjects. They are used to distinguish between two types of quantities being considered, separating them into those available at the start of a process and those being created by it, where the latter (dependent variables) are dependent on the former (independent variables.)

   In traditional calculus, a function is defined as a relation between two terms called variables because their values vary.

   a. BDDC
   b. 15 theorem
   c. BIBO stability
   d. Dependent variable

Chapter 9. POLAR COORDINATES AND PARAMETRIC CURVES

6. In calculus, a branch of mathematics, the _____ is a measurement of how a function changes when its input changes. Loosely speaking, a _____ can be thought of as how much a quantity is changing at some given point. For example, the _____ of the position (or distance) of a vehicle with respect to time is the instantaneous velocity (respectively, instantaneous speed) at which the vehicle is traveling.

The process of finding a _____ is called differentiation. The fundamental theorem of calculus states that differentiation is the reverse process to integration.

    a. Stationary phase approximation   b. Semi-differentiability
    c. Bounded function   d. Derivative

7. In mathematics, the _____ is a two-dimensional coordinate system in which each point on a plane is determined by an angle and a distance. The _____ is especially useful in situations where the relationship between two points is most easily expressed in terms of angles and distance; in the more familiar Cartesian or rectangular coordinate system, such a relationship can only be found through trigonometric formulation.

As the coordinate system is two-dimensional, each point is determined by two polar coordinates: the radial coordinate and the angular coordinate.

    a. BDDC   b. 15 theorem
    c. BIBO stability   d. Polar coordinate system

8. In mathematics and its applications, a _____ system is a system for assigning an n-tuple of numbers or scalars to each point in an n-dimensional space. This concept is part of the theory of manifolds. 'Scalars' in many cases means real numbers, but, depending on context, can mean complex numbers or elements of some other commutative ring.

    a. 15 theorem   b. Coordinate
    c. Spherical coordinate system   d. Cylindrical coordinate system

9. In complex analysis, a mathematical discipline, a _____ of a meromorphic function is a certain type of singularity that behaves like the singularity of $\frac{1}{z^n}$ at z = 0. This means that, in particular, a _____ of the function f(z) is a point z = a such that f(z) approaches infinity uniformly as z approaches a.

Formally, suppose U is an open subset of the complex plane C, a is an element of U and f : U {a} → C is a function which is holomorphic over its domain.

    a. Lacunary function   b. Complex logarithm
    c. Bieberbach conjecture   d. Pole

10. A _____ is closed curve with one cusp.

In geometry, the _____ is an epicycloid with one cusp.

Rolling circle around another fixed circle produces _____ (red curve) Conformal mapping from circle to _____

- epicycloid produced as the path (or locus) of a point on the circumference of a circle as that circle rolls around another fixed circle with the same radius.

- limaçon with one cusp. The cusp is formed when the ratio of a to b in the equation is equal to one.

- a. BDDC
- b. Cardioid
- c. 15 theorem
- d. BIBO stability

11. In mathematics, a _____ or rhodonea curve is a sinusoid plotted in polar coordinates. Up to similarity, these curves can all be expressed by a polar equation of the form

$$r = \cos(k\theta).$$

If k is an integer, the curve will be _____ shaped with

- 2k petals if k is even, and
- k petals if k is odd.

When k is even, the entire graph of the _____ will be traced out exactly once when the value of θ changes from 0 to 2π. When k is odd, this will happen on the interval between 0 and π. (More generally, this will happen on any interval of length 2π for k even, and π for k odd.)

- a. Rose
- b. Space curve
- c. Cochleoid
- d. Curtate cycloid

12. In mathematics, a (topological) _____ is defined as follows: let I be an interval of real numbers (i.e. a non-empty connected subset of $\mathbb{R}$); then a _____ γ is a continuous mapping $\gamma : I \to X$, where X is a topological space. The _____ γ is said to be simple if it is injective, i.e. if for all x, y in I, we have $\gamma(x) = \gamma(y) \implies x = y$. If I is a closed bounded interval $[a, b]$, we also allow the possibility $\gamma(a) = \gamma(b)$ (this convention makes it possible to talk about closed simple _____.)

- a. Prolate cycloid
- b. Closed curve
- c. Tractrix
- d. Curve

13. In mathematics, _____ are a method of defining a curve. A simple kinematical example is when one uses a time parameter to determine the position, velocity, and other information about a body in motion.

Abstractly, a relation is given in the form of an equation, and it is shown also to be the image of functions from items such as R^n.

a. Critical point
b. Partial derivative
c. Shift theorem
d. Parametric equations

14. In mathematics, a _____ is the graph of the system of parametric equations

$$x = A\sin(at + \delta), \quad y = B\sin(bt),$$

which describes complex harmonic motion. This family of curves was investigated by Nathaniel Bowditch in 1815, and later in more detail by Jules Antoine Lissajous in 1857.

The appearance of the figure is highly sensitive to the ratio a/b.

a. Lissajous curve
b. BIBO stability
c. BDDC
d. 15 theorem

15. A _____ is the curve defined by the path of a point on the edge of circular wheel as the wheel rolls along a straight line. It is an example of a roulette, a curve generated by a curve rolling on another curve.

The _____ is the solution to the brachistochrone problem (i.e. it is the curve of fastest descent under gravity) and the related tautochrone problem (i.e. the period of a ball rolling back and forth inside it does not depend on the ball's starting position.)

a. Curtate cycloid
b. Tractrix
c. Prolate cycloid
d. Cycloid

16. A _____ is the curve between two points that is covered in the least time by a body that starts at the first point with zero speed and is constrained to move along the curve to the second point, under the action of constant gravity and assuming no friction.

Given two points A and B, with A not lower than B, there is just one upside down cycloid that passes through A with infinite slope, passes also through B and does not have maximum points between A and B. This particular inverted cycloid is a _____. The curve does not depend on the body's mass or on the strength of the gravitational constant.

a. Prolate cycloid
b. Space curve
c. Brachistochrone curve
d. Closed curve

17. In Geometry, the _____ is an algebraic curve defined by the equation

$$x^3 + y^3 - 3axy = 0.$$

It forms a loop in the first quadrant with a double point at the origin and asymptote

$$x + y + a = 0$$

It is symmetrical about y = x.

   a. Cochleoid
   c. Prolate cycloid
   b. Folium of Descartes
   d. Curve

18. _____ is the word created by Gilles de Roberval for the curve described by a fixed point as a circle rolls along a straight line. As a circle of radius a rolls without slipping along a line L, the center C moves parallel to L, and every other point P in the rotating plane rigidly attached to the circle traces the curve called the _____. Let CP = b. If P lies inside the circle (b < a), on its circumference (b = a), or outside (b > a), the _____ is described as being curtate, common, or prolate, respectively.

   a. Hypocycloid
   c. Kappa curve
   b. Witch of Agnesi
   d. Trochoid

19. A _____ is a surface created by rotating a curve lying on some plane (the generatrix) around a straight line (the axis of rotation) that lies on the same plane.

Examples of surfaces generated by a straight line are the cylindrical and conical surfaces. A circle that is rotated about a (coplanar) axis through the center generates a sphere.

   a. Riemann sum
   c. Surface of revolution
   b. Shell integration
   d. Constant of integration

20. The _____ of any solid, liquid, plasma, vacuum or theoretical object is how much three-dimensional space it occupies, often quantified numerically. One-dimensional figures (such as lines) and two-dimensional shapes (such as squares) are assigned zero _____ in the three-dimensional space. _____ is commonly presented in units such as mL or cm^3 (milliliters or cubic centimeters.)

   a. Klein-Gordon equation
   c. Dirac equation
   b. Volume
   d. Vector potential

21. In a totally ordered set all elements are mutually comparable, so such a set can have at most one minimal element and at most one maximal element. Then, due to mutual comparability, the minimal element will also be the least element and the maximal element will also be the greatest element. Thus in a totally ordered set we can simply use the terms minimum and _____.

   a. Leibniz rule
   c. Maximum
   b. Racetrack principle
   d. Nth term

22. In a totally ordered set all elements are mutually comparable, so such a set can have at most one minimal element and at most one maximal element. Then, due to mutual comparability, the minimal element will also be the least element and the maximal element will also be the greatest element. Thus in a totally ordered set we can simply use the terms _____ and maximum.

a. Ghosts of departed quantities
c. Minimum
b. Nth term
d. Maximum

23. In geometry, a _____ (pl. tori) is a surface of revolution generated by revolving a circle in three dimensional space about an axis coplanar with the circle, which does not touch the circle. Examples of tori include the surfaces of doughnuts and inner tubes.
    a. Hyperbolic paraboloid
    b. Prolate
    c. Paraboloid
    d. Torus

24. _____ is any physical or virtual entity that is owned by an individual or jointly by a group of individuals. An owner of _____ has the right to consume, sell, rent, mortgage, transfer and exchange his or her _____. Important widely-recognized types of _____ include real _____, personal _____ (other physical possessions), and intellectual _____ (rights over artistic creations, inventions, etc.), although the latter is not always as widely recognized or enforced.
    a. 15 theorem
    b. BDDC
    c. BIBO stability
    d. Property

25. In mathematics, a _____ is a function which preserves the given order. This concept first arose in calculus, and was later generalized to the more abstract setting of order theory.

In calculus, a function f defined on a subset of the real numbers with real values is called monotonic (also monotonically increasing or non-decreasing), if for all x and y such that x >≤ y one has f(x) >≤ f(y), so f preserves the order.

    a. Pseudo-differential operator
    b. 15 theorem
    c. Pettis integral
    d. Monotonic function

26. In mathematics, the _____ of a function is the set of all 'output' values produced by that function. Sometimes it is called the image, or more precisely, the image of the domain of the function. If a function is a surjection then its _____ is equal to its codomain.
    a. Surjective
    b. Constant function
    c. Piecewise-defined function
    d. Range

27. Integration is an important concept in mathematics, specifically in the field of calculus and, more broadly, mathematical analysis. Given a function f of a real variable x and an interval [a, b] of the real line, the _____

$$\int_a^b f(x)\,dx,$$

is defined informally to be the net signed area of the region in the xy-plane bounded by the graph of f, the x-axis, and the vertical lines x = a and x = b.

The term '_____' may also refer to the notion of antiderivative, a function F whose derivative is the given function f.

a. Indefinite integral
c. Integral test for convergence
b. Integral
d. Integrand

28. In mathematics, the concept of a '_____' is used to describe the behavior of a function as its argument or input either 'gets close' to some point, or as the argument becomes arbitrarily large; or the behavior of a sequence's elements as their index increases indefinitely. Limits are used in calculus and other branches of mathematical analysis to define derivatives and continuity.

In formulas, _____ is usually abbreviated as lim

a. BIBO stability
c. 15 theorem
b. BDDC
d. Limit

29. Call S_N the _____ to N of the sequence {a_n}, or _____ of the series. A series is the sequence of partial sums, {S_N}.

When talking about series, one can refer either to the sequence {S_N} of the partial sums, or to the sum of the series,

$$\sum_{n=0}^{\infty} a_n$$

i.e., the limit of the sequence of partial sums - it is clear which one is meant from context.

a. Dirichlet integral
c. Partial sum
b. Maxima
d. The Method of Mechanical Theorems

30. In mathematics, the _____, sometimes called the direct _____ is a criterion for convergence or divergence of a series whose terms are real or complex numbers. The test determines convergence by comparing the terms of the series in question with those of a series whose convergence properties are known.

The _____ states that if the series

$$\sum_{n=1}^{\infty} b_n$$

is an absolutely convergent series and

$$|a_n| \leq |b_n|$$

Chapter 9. POLAR COORDINATES AND PARAMETRIC CURVES

for sufficiently large n , then the series

$$\sum_{n=1}^{\infty} a_n$$

converges absolutely.

    a. Telescoping series
    b. Conditionally convergent
    c. Ratio test
    d. Comparison test

31.   Cantor defined two kinds of _____ numbers, the ordinal numbers and the cardinal numbers. Ordinal numbers may be identified with well-ordered sets, or counting carried on to any stopping point, including points after an _____ number have already been counted. Generalizing finite and the ordinary _____ sequences which are maps from the positive integers leads to mappings from ordinal numbers, and transfinite sequences.
    a. ALGOR
    b. ACTRAN
    c. AUSM
    d. Infinite

32.   The terms of the series are often produced according to a certain rule, such as by a formula, by an algorithm, by a sequence of measurements, or even by a random number generator. As there are an infinite number of terms, this notion is often called an _____. Unlike finite summations, series need tools from mathematical analysis to be fully understood and manipulated.
    a. Infinite series
    b. Integration by substitution
    c. Extreme Value Theorem
    d. Extreme value

33.   In mathematics, the _____ for convergence is a method used to test infinite series of non-negative terms for convergence. An early form of the test of convergence was developed in India by Madhava in the 14th century, and by his followers at the Kerala School. In Europe, it was later developed by Maclaurin and Cauchy and is sometimes known as the Maclaurin-Cauchy test.
    a. ACTRAN
    b. ALGOR
    c. Integral test
    d. AUSM

34.   If a function has an integral, it is said to be integrable. The function for which the integral is calculated is called the _____. The region over which a function is being integrated is called the domain of integration.
    a. Integration by parts
    b. Integrand
    c. Integral test for convergence
    d. Order of integration

35.   An _____ of a real-valued function y = f(x) is a curve which describes the behavior of f as either x or y tends to infinity.

In other words, as one moves along the graph of f(x) in some direction, the distance between it and the _____ eventually becomes smaller than any distance that one may specify.

a. ALGOR
b. ACTRAN
c. Asymptote
d. AUSM

Chapter 10. INFINITE SERIES

1. In mathematics, a _____ is an ordered list of objects (or events). Like a set, it contains members (also called elements or terms), and the number of terms (possibly infinite) is called the length of the _____. Unlike a set, order matters, and the exact same elements can appear multiple times at different positions in the _____.
   a. Y-intercept
   b. Sequence
   c. 15 theorem
   d. Slope

2. Cantor defined two kinds of _____ numbers, the ordinal numbers and the cardinal numbers. Ordinal numbers may be identified with well-ordered sets, or counting carried on to any stopping point, including points after an _____ number have already been counted. Generalizing finite and the ordinary _____ sequences which are maps from the positive integers leads to mappings from ordinal numbers, and transfinite sequences.
   a. ACTRAN
   b. ALGOR
   c. AUSM
   d. Infinite

3. In mathematics, the _____ test for divergence is a simple test for the divergence of an infinite series:

   - If $\lim_{n \to \infty} a_n \neq 0$ or if the limit does not exist, then $\sum_{n=1}^{\infty} a_n$ diverges.

Many authors do not name this test or give it a shorter name.

Unlike stronger convergence tests, the term test cannot prove by itself that a series converges. In particular, the converse to the test is not true; instead all one can say is:

   - If $\lim_{n \to \infty} a_n = 0$, then $\sum_{n=1}^{\infty} a_n$ may or may not converge. In other words, if $\lim_{n \to \infty} a_n = 0$, the test is inconclusive.

The harmonic series is a classic example of a divergent series whose terms limit to zero. The more general class of p-series,

$$\sum_{n=1}^{\infty} \frac{1}{n^p},$$

exemplifies the possible results of the test:

   - If $p \leq 0$, then the term test identifies the series as divergent.
   - If $0 < p \leq 1$, then the term test is inconclusive, but the series is divergent by the integral test for convergence.
   - If $1 < p$, then the term test is inconclusive, but the series is convergent, again by the integral test for convergence.

The test is typically proved in contrapositive form:

- If $\sum_{n=1}^{\infty} a_n$ converges, then $\lim_{n \to \infty} a_n = 0$.

If s_n are the partial sums of the series, then the assumption that the series converges means that

$$\lim_{n \to \infty} s_n = s$$

for some number s. Then

$$\lim_{n \to \infty} a_n = \lim_{n \to \infty} (s_n - s_{n-1}) = s - s = 0.$$

The assumption that the series converges means that it passes Cauchy's convergence test: for every $\varepsilon > 0$ there is a number N such that

$$|a_{n+1} + a_{n+2} + \ldots + a_{n+p}| < \varepsilon$$

holds for all n > N and p ≥ 1. Setting p = 1 recovers the definition of the statement

$$\lim_{n \to \infty} a_n = 0.$$

The simplest version of the term test applies to infinite series of real numbers.

a. Minimum
b. Slope field
c. Leibniz differential
d. Nth term

4. A _____ is perfectly round geometrical object in three-dimensional space, such as the shape of a round ball. Like a circle in two dimensions, a perfect _____ is completely symmetrical around its center, with all points on the surface lying the same distance r from the center point. This distance r is known as the radius of the _____.
   a. North pole
   b. Tangent line
   c. Minimal surface
   d. Sphere

5. If a particular point on a sphere is (arbitrarily) designated as its _____, then the corresponding antipodal point is called the south pole and the equator is the great circle that is equidistant to them. Great circles through the two poles are called lines (or meridians) of longitude, and the line connecting the two poles is called the axis of rotation. Circles on the sphere that are parallel to the equator are lines of latitude.
   a. Sphere
   b. North pole
   c. Tangent line
   d. Minimal surface

Chapter 10. INFINITE SERIES

6. In mathematics and its applications, a _____ system is a system for assigning an n-tuple of numbers or scalars to each point in an n-dimensional space. This concept is part of the theory of manifolds. 'Scalars' in many cases means real numbers, but, depending on context, can mean complex numbers or elements of some other commutative ring.
   a. Spherical coordinate system
   b. 15 theorem
   c. Cylindrical coordinate system
   d. Coordinate

7. In mathematics, the concept of a '_____' is used to describe the behavior of a function as its argument or input either 'gets close' to some point, or as the argument becomes arbitrarily large; or the behavior of a sequence's elements as their index increases indefinitely. Limits are used in calculus and other branches of mathematical analysis to define derivatives and continuity.

   In formulas, _____ is usually abbreviated as lim

   a. BIBO stability
   b. Limit
   c. 15 theorem
   d. BDDC

8. Integration is an important concept in mathematics, specifically in the field of calculus and, more broadly, mathematical analysis. Given a function f of a real variable x and an interval [a, b] of the real line, the _____

$$\int_a^b f(x)\,dx,$$

   is defined informally to be the net signed area of the region in the xy-plane bounded by the graph of f, the x-axis, and the vertical lines x = a and x = b.

   The term '_____' may also refer to the notion of antiderivative, a function F whose derivative is the given function f.

   a. Indefinite integral
   b. Integral
   c. Integral test for convergence
   d. Integrand

9. In mathematics, the _____ for convergence is a method used to test infinite series of non-negative terms for convergence. An early form of the test of convergence was developed in India by Madhava in the 14th century, and by his followers at the Kerala School. In Europe, it was later developed by Maclaurin and Cauchy and is sometimes known as the Maclaurin-Cauchy test.
   a. AUSM
   b. ALGOR
   c. Integral test
   d. ACTRAN

10. The most commonly encountered form of Hooke's law is probably the spring equation, which relates the force exerted by a spring to the distance it is stretched by a _____, k, measured in force per length.

$$F = -kx$$

The negative sign indicates that the force exerted by the spring is in direct opposition to the direction of displacement. It is called a 'restoring force', as it tends to restore the system to equilibrium.

Chapter 10. INFINITE SERIES

a. Navier-Stokes equations
c. Spring constant
b. Polar moment of inertia
d. Spring equation

11. _____ is a type of motion in which the velocity of an object changes equal amounts in equal time periods. An example of an object having _____ would be a ball rolling down a ramp. The object picks up velocity as it goes down the ramp with equal changes in time.
  a. AUSM
  b. Uniform Acceleration
  c. ACTRAN
  d. ALGOR

12. In mathematics, a function f defined on some set X with real or complex values is a _____ function, if the set of its values is _____. In other words, there exists a number M>0 such that

$$|f(x)| \leq M$$

for all x in X.

Sometimes, if $f(x) \leq A$ for all x in X, then the function is said to be _____ above by A.

  a. Bounded
  b. Stationary phase approximation
  c. Differential coefficient
  d. Concave upwards

13. In mathematics, a real-valued function f defined on an interval (or on any convex subset of some vector space) is called convex, _____, concave up or convex cup, if for any two points x and y in its domain C and any t in [0,1], we have

$$f(tx + (1-t)y) \leq tf(x) + (1-t)f(y).$$

Convex function on an interval.

In other words, a function is convex if and only if its epigraph (the set of points lying on or above the graph) is a convex set.

Pictorially, a function is called 'convex' if the function lies below the straight line segment connecting two points, for any two points in the interval.

A function is called strictly convex if

$$f(tx + (1-t)y) < tf(x) + (1-t)f(y)$$

for any t in (0,1) and $x \neq y$.

A function f is said to be concave if − f is convex.

a. Mountain pass theorem
c. Concave upwards
b. Vertical asymptote
d. Third derivative

14. In mathematics, especially in order theory, an _____ of a subset S of some partially ordered set (P, >≤) is an element of P which is greater than or equal to every element of S. The term lower bound is defined dually as an element of P which is lesser than or equal to every element of S. A set with an _____ is said to be bounded from above by that bound, a set with a lower bound is said to be bounded from below by that bound.

A subset S of a partially ordered set P may fail to have any bounds or may have many different upper and lower bounds. By transitivity, any element greater than or equal to an _____ of S is again an _____ of S, and any element lesser than or equal to any lower bound of S is again a lower bound of S. This leads to the consideration of least upper bounds: (or suprema) and greatest lower bounds (or infima.)

a. Upper bound
c. AUSM
b. ACTRAN
d. ALGOR

15. A _____ is a statement of the meaning of a word or phrase. The term to be defined is known as the definiendum . The words which define it are known as the definiens .
a. BIBO stability
c. 15 theorem
b. BDDC
d. Definition

16. In mathematics, a _____ is a function which preserves the given order. This concept first arose in calculus, and was later generalized to the more abstract setting of order theory.

In calculus, a function f defined on a subset of the real numbers with real values is called monotonic (also monotonically increasing or non-decreasing), if for all x and y such that x >≤ y one has f(x) >≤ f(y), so f preserves the order.

a. 15 theorem
c. Monotonic function
b. Pseudo-differential operator
d. Pettis integral

17. _____ is any physical or virtual entity that is owned by an individual or jointly by a group of individuals. An owner of _____ has the right to consume, sell, rent, mortgage, transfer and exchange his or her _____. Important widely-recognized types of _____ include real _____, personal _____ (other physical possessions), and intellectual _____ (rights over artistic creations, inventions, etc.), although the latter is not always as widely recognized or enforced.
a. BIBO stability
c. BDDC
b. Property
d. 15 theorem

18. A _____ is a surface created by rotating a curve lying on some plane (the generatrix) around a straight line (the axis of rotation) that lies on the same plane.

Examples of surfaces generated by a straight line are the cylindrical and conical surfaces. A circle that is rotated about a (coplanar) axis through the center generates a sphere.

Chapter 10. INFINITE SERIES

a. Shell integration
b. Riemann sum
c. Constant of integration
d. Surface of revolution

19. In calculus, interchange of the _____ is a methodology that transforms multiple integrations of functions into other, hopefully simpler, integrals by changing the order in which the integrations are performed.

The problem for examination is evaluation of an integral of the form:

$$\iint_D dxdy\, f(x,y),$$

where D is some two-dimensional area in the xy-plane. For some functions f straightforward integration is feasible, but where that is not true, the integral can sometimes be reduced to simpler form by changing the _____.

a. Order of integration
b. Indefinite integral
c. Integration by parts
d. Arc length

20. Call S_N the _____ to N of the sequence {a_n}, or _____ of the series. A series is the sequence of partial sums, {S_N}.

When talking about series, one can refer either to the sequence {S_N} of the partial sums, or to the sum of the series,

$$\sum_{n=0}^{\infty} a_n$$

i.e., the limit of the sequence of partial sums - it is clear which one is meant from context.

a. Dirichlet integral
b. The Method of Mechanical Theorems
c. Maxima
d. Partial sum

21. In mathematics, a _____ is a series with a constant ratio between successive terms. For example, the series

$$\frac{1}{2} + \frac{1}{4} + \frac{1}{8} + \frac{1}{16} + \cdots$$

is geometric, because each term is equal to half of the previous term. The sum of this series is 1, as illustrated in the following picture:

_____ are one of the simplest examples of infinite series with finite sums.

a. Converge absolutely
b. Sequence transformation
c. Conditionally convergent
d. Geometric series

22. In mathematics, a _____ is a method for approximating the total area underneath a curve on a graph, otherwise known as an integral. It may also be used to define the integration operation.

Consider a function $f: D \rightarrow \mathbf{R}$, where D is a subset of the real numbers $\mathbf{R}$, and let $I = [a, b]$ be a closed interval contained in D. A finite set of points $\{x_0, x_1, x_2, \ldots x_n\}$ such that $a = x_0 < x_1 < x_2 \ldots < x_n = b$ creates a partition

$$P = \{[x_0, x_1), [x_1, x_2), \ldots [x_{n-1}, x_n]\}$$

of I.

a. Risch algorithm
b. Riemann sum
c. Signed measure
d. Solid of revolution

23. In vector calculus, the _____ is an operator that measures the magnitude of a vector field's source or sink at a given point; the _____ of a vector field is a (signed) scalar. For example, consider air as it is heated or cooled. The relevant vector field for this example is the velocity of the moving air at a point.

a. Triple product
b. Green's theorem
c. Gradient theorem
d. Divergence

24. In mathematics, the nth term _____ is a simple test for the divergence of an infinite series:

- If $\lim_{n \to \infty} a_n \neq 0$ or if the limit does not exist, then $\sum_{n=1}^{\infty} a_n$ diverges.

Many authors do not name this test or give it a shorter name.

Unlike stronger convergence tests, the term test cannot prove by itself that a series converges. In particular, the converse to the test is not true; instead all one can say is:

- If $\lim_{n \to \infty} a_n = 0$, then $\sum_{n=1}^{\infty} a_n$ may or may not converge. In other words, if $\lim_{n \to \infty} a_n = 0$, the test is inconclusive.

The harmonic series is a classic example of a divergent series whose terms limit to zero. The more general class of p-series,

$$\sum_{n=1}^{\infty} \frac{1}{n^p},$$

exemplifies the possible results of the test:

- If p ≤ 0, then the term test identifies the series as divergent.
- If 0 < p ≤ 1, then the term test is inconclusive, but the series is divergent by the integral test for convergence.
- If 1 < p, then the term test is inconclusive, but the series is convergent, again by the integral test for convergence.

The test is typically proved in contrapositive form:

- If $\sum_{n=1}^{\infty} a_n$ converges, then $\lim_{n \to \infty} a_n = 0$.

If s_n are the partial sums of the series, then the assumption that the series converges means that

$$\lim_{n \to \infty} s_n = s$$

for some number s. Then

$$\lim_{n \to \infty} a_n = \lim_{n \to \infty} (s_n - s_{n-1}) = s - s = 0.$$

The assumption that the series converges means that it passes Cauchy's convergence test: for every $\varepsilon > 0$ there is a number N such that

$$|a_{n+1} + a_{n+2} + \ldots + a_{n+p}| < \varepsilon$$

holds for all n > N and p ≥ 1. Setting p = 1 recovers the definition of the statement

$$\lim_{n \to \infty} a_n = 0.$$

The simplest version of the term test applies to infinite series of real numbers.

a. Test for divergence
b. Fundamental Theorem of Calculus
c. Calculus controversy
d. Leibniz differential

25. In acoustics and telecommunication, a _____ of a wave is a component frequency of the signal that is an integer multiple of the fundamental frequency. For example, if the fundamental frequency is f, the harmonics have frequencies f, 2f, 3f, 4f, etc. The harmonics have the property that they are all periodic at the fundamental frequency, therefore the sum of harmonics is also periodic at that frequency.

a. BIBO stability b. BDDC
c. 15 theorem d. Harmonic

26. In mathematics, the _____ is the infinite series

$$\sum_{k=1}^{\infty} \frac{1}{k} = 1 + \frac{1}{2} + \frac{1}{3} + \frac{1}{4} + \cdots.$$

Its name derives from the concept of overtones, or harmonics, in music: the wavelengths of the overtones of a vibrating string are 1/2, 1/3, 1/4, etc., of the string's fundamental wavelength. Every term of the series after the first is the harmonic mean of the neighboring terms; the term harmonic mean likewise derives from music.

The _____ diverges to infinity, albeit rather slowly (the first 10^{43} terms sum to less than 100 .)

a. Harmonic series b. 15 theorem
c. BIBO stability d. BDDC

27. _____ is the long dimension of any object. The _____ of a thing is the distance between its ends, its linear extent as measured from end to end. This may be distinguished from height, which is vertical extent, and width or breadth, which are the distance from side to side, measuring across the object at right angles to the _____.

a. Length b. BDDC
c. BIBO stability d. 15 theorem

28. In mathematics, _____ refers to the rewriting of an expression into a simpler form. For example, the process of rewriting a fraction into one with the smallest whole-number denominator possible (while keeping the numerator an integer) is called 'reducing a fraction'. Rewriting a radical (or 'root') expression with the smallest possible whole number under the radical symbol is called 'reducing a radical'.

a. Quartic b. Reduction
c. 15 theorem d. BDDC

29. _____ is how much exposed area an object has. It is expressed in square units. If an object has flat faces, its _____ can be calculated by adding together the areas of its faces.

a. Surface area b. Lipschitz domain
c. Plane curve d. Vector area

30. The terms of the series are often produced according to a certain rule, such as by a formula, by an algorithm, by a sequence of measurements, or even by a random number generator. As there are an infinite number of terms, this notion is often called an _____. Unlike finite summations, series need tools from mathematical analysis to be fully understood and manipulated.

a. Extreme value b. Extreme Value Theorem
c. Infinite series d. Integration by substitution

31. In geometry, a _____ (pl. tori) is a surface of revolution generated by revolving a circle in three dimensional space about an axis coplanar with the circle, which does not touch the circle. Examples of tori include the surfaces of doughnuts and inner tubes.

a. Paraboloid
b. Hyperbolic paraboloid
c. Torus
d. Prolate

32. A surface normal to a flat surface is a vector which is perpendicular to that surface. A normal to a non-flat surface at a point P on the surface is a vector perpendicular to the tangent plane to that surface at P. The word 'normal' is also used as an adjective: a line normal to a plane, the normal component of a force, the _____, etc. The concept of normality generalizes to orthogonality.
   a. Hyperbolic paraboloid
   b. Paraboloid
   c. Normal line
   d. Normal vector

33. In calculus, _____ gives a sequence of approximations of a differentiable function around a given point by polynomials (the Taylor polynomials of that function) whose coefficients depend only on the derivatives of the function at that point. The theorem also gives precise estimates on the size of the error in the approximation. The theorem is named after the mathematician Brook Taylor, who stated it in 1712, though the result was first discovered 41 years earlier in 1671 by James Gregory.
   a. Fresnel integrals
   b. Related rates
   c. Local minimum
   d. Taylor's theorem

34. In elementary mathematics, physics, and engineering, a _____ is a geometric object that has both a magnitude (or length), direction and sense, (i.e., orientation along the given direction.) A _____ is frequently represented by a line segment with a definite direction, or graphically as an arrow, connecting an initial point A with a terminal point B, and denoted by

The magnitude of the _____ is the length of the segment and the direction characterizes the displacement of B relative to A: how much one should move the point A to 'carry' it to the point B.

Many algebraic operations on real numbers have close analogues for vectors.

   a. Vector
   b. 15 theorem
   c. Linear partial differential operator
   d. BDDC

35. In mathematics, the _____ is a representation of a function as an infinite sum of terms calculated from the values of its derivatives at a single point. It may be regarded as the limit of the Taylor polynomials. If the series is centered at zero, the series is also called a Maclaurin series.
   a. 15 theorem
   b. BIBO stability
   c. Taylor series
   d. BDDC

36. In a totally ordered set all elements are mutually comparable, so such a set can have at most one minimal element and at most one maximal element. Then, due to mutual comparability, the minimal element will also be the least element and the maximal element will also be the greatest element. Thus in a totally ordered set we can simply use the terms minimum and _____.

a. Maximum
b. Leibniz rule
c. Racetrack principle
d. Nth term

37. In a totally ordered set all elements are mutually comparable, so such a set can have at most one minimal element and at most one maximal element. Then, due to mutual comparability, the minimal element will also be the least element and the maximal element will also be the greatest element. Thus in a totally ordered set we can simply use the terms _____ and maximum.

   a. Nth term
   b. Maximum
   c. Ghosts of departed quantities
   d. Minimum

38. In mathematics, a _____ is any function which can be written as the ratio of two polynomial functions.

$$y = \frac{x^2 - 3x - 2}{x^2 - 4}$$

In the case of one variable, x, a _____ is a function of the form

$$f(x) = \frac{P(x)}{Q(x)}$$

where P and Q are polynomial function in x and Q is not the zero polynomial. The domain of f is the set of all points x for which the denominator Q(x) is not zero.

   a. 15 theorem
   b. BIBO stability
   c. BDDC
   d. Rational function

39. _____ generally conveys two primary meanings. The first is an imprecise sense of harmonious or aesthetically-pleasing proportionality and balance; such that it reflects beauty or perfection. The second meaning is a precise and well-defined concept of balance or 'patterned self-similarity' that can be demonstrated or proved according to the rules of a formal system: by geometry, through physics or otherwise.

   a. 15 theorem
   b. BIBO stability
   c. BDDC
   d. Symmetry

40. In mathematics, the _____ is a two-dimensional coordinate system in which each point on a plane is determined by an angle and a distance. The _____ is especially useful in situations where the relationship between two points is most easily expressed in terms of angles and distance; in the more familiar Cartesian or rectangular coordinate system, such a relationship can only be found through trigonometric formulation.

As the coordinate system is two-dimensional, each point is determined by two polar coordinates: the radial coordinate and the angular coordinate.

   a. 15 theorem
   b. BDDC
   c. BIBO stability
   d. Polar coordinate system

Chapter 10. INFINITE SERIES

41. In mathematics, the _____, named after German mathematician Bernhard Riemann, is a prominent function of great significance in number theory because of its relation to the distribution of prime numbers. It also has applications in other areas such as physics, probability theory, and applied statistics.

The Riemann hypothesis, a conjecture about the distribution of the zeros of the _____, is considered by many mathematicians to be the most important unsolved problem in pure mathematics.

a. 15 theorem
c. Riemann zeta function
b. BIBO stability
d. BDDC

42. In mathematics, a _____ (or just conic) is a curve obtained by intersecting a cone (more precisely, a circular conical surface) with a plane. A _____ is therefore a restriction of a quadric surface to the plane. The conic sections were named and studied as long ago as 200 BC, when Apollonius of Perga undertook a systematic study of their properties.

a. Latus rectum
c. 15 theorem
b. Conic section
d. BDDC

43. In mathematics, the _____, sometimes called the direct _____ is a criterion for convergence or divergence of a series whose terms are real or complex numbers. The test determines convergence by comparing the terms of the series in question with those of a series whose convergence properties are known.

The _____ states that if the series

$$\sum_{n=1}^{\infty} b_n$$

is an absolutely convergent series and

$$|a_n| \leq |b_n|$$

for sufficiently large n, then the series

$$\sum_{n=1}^{\infty} a_n$$

converges absolutely.

a. Ratio test
c. Conditionally convergent
b. Telescoping series
d. Comparison test

44. The _____ converges:

$$\sum_{k=1}^{\infty} \frac{(-1)^{k+1}}{k} = 1 - \frac{1}{2} + \frac{1}{3} - \frac{1}{4} + \cdots = \ln 2 = 0.693\,147\,180\ldots.$$

This equality is a consequence of the Mercator series, the Taylor series for the natural logarithm. Another equality, similar in form to Mercator's series, is:

$$\sum_{k=0}^{\infty} \frac{(-1)^k}{2k+1} = 1 - \frac{1}{3} + \frac{1}{5} - \frac{1}{7} + \cdots = \arctan(1) = \frac{\pi}{4}.$$

This is a consequence of the Taylor series representation of the inverse tangent function (which has a radius of convergence of 1.)

The nth partial sum of the diverging harmonic series,

$$H_n = \sum_{k=1}^{n} \frac{1}{k},$$

is called the nth harmonic number.

a. AUSM
b. Alternating harmonic series
c. ACTRAN
d. ALGOR

45. In mathematics, an _____ is an infinite series of the form

$$\sum_{n=0}^{\infty} (-1)^n a_n,$$

with $a_n \geq 0$ (or $a_n \leq 0$) for all n. A finite sum of this kind is an alternating sum. An _____ converges if the terms a_n converge to 0 monotonically.

a. Extreme value
b. Infinite series
c. Uniform convergence
d. Alternating series

46. The _____ is a method used to prove that infinite series of terms converge. It was discovered by Gottfried Leibniz and is sometimes known as Leibniz's test or the Leibniz criterion.

A series of the form

$$\sum_{n=1}^{\infty} (-1)^n a_n$$

where all the a_n are positive or 0, is called an alternating series.

Chapter 10. INFINITE SERIES

a. Eisenstein series
b. Absolute convergence
c. ACTRAN
d. Alternating series test

47. In geometry, the _____, geometric center, or barycenter of a plane figure X is the intersection of all straight lines that divide X into two parts of equal moment about the line. Informally, it is the 'average' of all points of X. The definition extends to any object X in n-dimensional space: its _____ is the intersection of all hyperplanes that divide X into two parts of equal moment.

a. BDDC
b. 15 theorem
c. BIBO stability
d. Centroid

48. In mathematics, a series (or sometimes also an integral) is said to converge absolutely if the sum (or integral) of the absolute value of the summand or integrand is finite.

More precisely, a real or complex-valued series $\sum_{n=0}^{\infty} a_n$ is said to converge absolutely if $\sum_{n=0}^{\infty} |a_n| < \infty$.

_____ is vitally important to the study of infinite series because on the one hand, it is strong enough that such series retain certain basic properties of finite sums -- the most important ones being rearrangement of the terms and convergence of products of two infinite series -- that are unfortunately not possessed by all convergent series. On the other hand _____ is weak enough to occur very often in practice.

a. Alternating series test
b. ACTRAN
c. Eisenstein series
d. Absolute convergence

49. In mathematics, a (topological) _____ is defined as follows: let I be an interval of real numbers (i.e. a non-empty connected subset of $\mathbb{R}$); then a _____ γ is a continuous mapping $\gamma : I \to X$, where X is a topological space. The _____ γ is said to be simple if it is injective, i.e. if for all x, y in I, we have $\gamma(x) = \gamma(y) \implies x = y$. If I is a closed bounded interval $[a, b]$, we also allow the possibility $\gamma(a) = \gamma(b)$ (this convention makes it possible to talk about closed simple _____.)

a. Tractrix
b. Closed curve
c. Prolate cycloid
d. Curve

50. In mathematics, a series or integral is said to be _____ if it converges, but it does not converge absolutely.

More precisely, a series $\sum_{n=0}^{\infty} a_n$ is said to converge conditionally if $\lim_{m \to \infty} \sum_{n=0}^{m} a_n$ exists and is a finite number (not ∞ or −∞), but $\sum_{n=0}^{\infty} |a_n| = \infty$.

Chapter 10. INFINITE SERIES

A classical example is given by

$$1 - \frac{1}{2} + \frac{1}{3} - \frac{1}{4} + \frac{1}{5} - \cdots = \sum_{n=1}^{\infty} \frac{(-1)^{n+1}}{n}$$

which converges to ln 2 , but is not absolutely convergent

The simplest examples of _____ series (including the one above) are the alternating series.

a. Ratio test
c. Geometric series
b. Converge absolutely
d. Conditionally convergent

51. In mathematics, a series (or sometimes also an integral) is said to _____ if the sum (or integral) of the absolute value of the summand or integrand is finite.

More precisely, a real or complex-valued series $\sum_{n=0}^{\infty} a_n$ is said to _____ if $\sum_{n=0}^{\infty} |a_n| < \infty$.

Absolute convergence is vitally important to the study of infinite series because on the one hand, it is strong enough that such series retain certain basic properties of finite sums -- the most important ones being rearrangement of the terms and convergence of products of two infinite series -- that are unfortunately not possessed by all convergent series. On the other hand absolute convergence is weak enough to occur very often in practice.

a. Sequence transformation
c. Converge absolutely
b. Ratio test
d. Telescoping series

52. A _____ is an expression which compares quantities relative to each other. The most common examples involve two quantities, but in theory any number of quantities can be compared. In mathematical terms, they are represented by separating each quantity with a colon, for example the _____ 2:3, which is read as the _____ 'two to three'.

a. Y-intercept
c. Sequence
b. 15 theorem
d. Ratio

53. In mathematics, the _____ is a test (or 'criterion') for the convergence of a series

$$\sum_{n=0}^{\infty} a_n$$

whose terms are real or complex numbers. The test was first published by Jean le Rond d'Alembert and is sometimes known as d'Alembert's _____. The test makes use of the number

()

in the cases where this limit exists.

- a. Geometric series
- b. Ratio test
- c. Converge absolutely
- d. Telescoping series

54. Continuous functions are of utmost importance in mathematics and applications. However, not all functions are continuous. If a function is not continuous at a point in its domain, one says that it has a _____ there. The set of all points of _____ of a function may be a discrete set, a dense set, or even the entire domain of the function.
- a. Discontinuity
- b. 15 theorem
- c. Vector
- d. BDDC

55. In mathematics, the _____ is a criterion for the convergence (a convergence test) of an infinite series

$$\sum_{n=1}^{\infty} a_n.$$

It is particularly useful in connection with power series.

The _____ was developed first by Cauchy and so is sometimes known as the Cauchy _____ or Cauchy's radical test.
The _____ uses the number

$$C = \limsup_{n \to \infty} \sqrt[n]{|a_n|},$$

where 'lim sup' denotes the limit superior, possibly ∞.

- a. Root test
- b. Racetrack principle
- c. Mean Value Theorem
- d. Related rates

56. In mathematics, a _____ (in one variable) is an infinite series of the form

$$f(x) = \sum_{n=0}^{\infty} a_n (x - c)^n = a_0 + a_1 (x - c)^1 + a_2 (x - c)^2 + a_3 (x - c)^3 + \cdots$$

where a_n represents the coefficient of the nth term, c is a constant, and x varies around c (for this reason one sometimes speaks of the series as being centered at c

In many situations c is equal to zero, for instance when considering a Maclaurin series.

a. Power series
b. Stationary phase approximation
c. Differential calculus
d. Differential coefficient

57. In mathematics, the _____ of a power series is a non-negative quantity, either a real number or ∞, that represents a domain (within the radius) in which the series will converge. Within the _____, a power series converges absolutely and uniformly on compacta as well. If the series converges, it is the Taylor series of the analytic function to which it converges inside its _____.

   a. Radius of convergence
   b. Branch point
   c. Blaschke product
   d. Holomorphically separable

58. In mathematics, _____, first defined by the mathematician Daniel Bernoulli and generalized by Friedrich Bessel, are canonical solutions y(x) of Bessel's differential equation:

$$x^2 \frac{d^2 y}{dx^2} + x \frac{dy}{dx} + (x^2 - \alpha^2) y = 0$$

for an arbitrary real or complex number α (the order of the Bessel function.) The most common and important special case is where α is an integer n.

Although α and −α produce the same differential equation, it is conventional to define different _____ for these two orders (e.g., so that the _____ are mostly smooth functions of α.)

   a. Bessel functions
   b. 15 theorem
   c. Logarithmic integral function
   d. Multiplication theorem

59. In elementary algebra, a _____ is a polynomial with two terms--the sum of two monomials--often bound by parenthesis or brackets when operated upon. It is the simplest kind of polynomial other than monomials.

- The _____ $a^2 - b^2$ can be factored as the product of two other binomials:

   $a^2 - b^2 = (a + b)(a - b.)$

   This is a special case of the more general formula:

   $$a^{n+1} - b^{n+1} = (a - b) \sum_{k=0}^{n} a^k b^{n-k}$$

- The product of a pair of linear binomials (ax + b) and (cx + d) is:

   $(ax + b)(cx + d) = acx^2 + axd + bcx + bd.$

- A _____ raised to the nth power, represented as

   $(a + b)^n$

   can be expanded by means of the _____ theorem or, equivalently, using Pascal's triangle. Taking a simple example, the perfect square _____ $(p + q)^2$ can be found by squaring the :first digit, adding twice the product of the first and second digit and finally adding the square of the second digit, to give $p^2 + 2pq + q^2$.

Chapter 10. INFINITE SERIES

    a. Binomial
    c. Multinomial theorem
    b. Completing the square
    d. Partial fractions

60. In mathematics, the _____ generalizes the purely algebraic formula of the binomial theorem to complex values of α. It is also a special case of a Newton series. The _____ is the series

$$(1+x)^\alpha = \sum_{k=0}^{\infty} \binom{\alpha}{k} x^k = \sum_{k=0}^{\infty} \frac{\prod_{a=0}^{k-1}(\alpha - a)\, x^k}{k!}$$

where α is a complex number and

$$\binom{\alpha}{k} = \frac{\alpha(\alpha-1)(\alpha-2)\cdots(\alpha-k+1)}{k!}$$

is the (generalized) binomial coefficient (if α is a non negative integer, then the (α + 1)th term and all later terms in the series are zero, since each one contains a factor equal to (α − α): thus, in that case, the summation reduces to the algebraic binomial formula.)

    a. Differential
    c. Maxima
    b. Fresnel integrals
    d. Binomial series

61. In calculus, a branch of mathematics, the _____ is a measurement of how a function changes when its input changes. Loosely speaking, a _____ can be thought of as how much a quantity is changing at some given point. For example, the _____ of the position (or distance) of a vehicle with respect to time is the instantaneous velocity (respectively, instantaneous speed) at which the vehicle is traveling.

The process of finding a _____ is called differentiation. The fundamental theorem of calculus states that differentiation is the reverse process to integration.

    a. Stationary phase approximation
    c. Derivative
    b. Bounded function
    d. Semi-differentiability

62. In geometry, the _____ (or simply the tangent) to a curve at a given point is the straight line that 'just touches' the curve at that point (in the sense explained more precisely below.) As it passes through the point of tangency, the _____ is 'going in the same direction' as the curve, and in this sense it is the best straight-line approximation to the curve at that point. The same definition applies to space curves and curves in n-dimensional Euclidean space.
    a. North pole
    c. Tangent line
    b. Lie derivative
    d. Minimal surface

63. In calculus and other branches of mathematical analysis, an _____ is an algebraic expression obtained in the context of limits. Limits involving algebraic operations are often performed by replacing subexpressions by their limits; if the expression obtained after this substitution does not give enough information to determine the original limit, it is known as an _____. The indeterminate forms include 0^0, 0/0, 1^∞, ∞ - ∞, ∞/∞, 0×∞, and ∞^0.

Chapter 10. INFINITE SERIES

 a. AUSM   b. ACTRAN
 c. ALGOR   d. Indeterminate form

64. In mathematics, the _____ is a binary operation on two vectors in a three-dimensional Euclidean space that results in another vector which is perpendicular to the plane containing the two input vectors. The algebra defined by the _____ is neither commutative nor associative. It contrasts with the dot product which produces a scalar result.

 a. Permutation   b. Cross product
 c. 15 theorem   d. Fundamental theorem of algebra

65. In infinitesimal calculus, a _____ is traditionally an infinitesimally small change in a variable. For example, if x is a variable, then a change in the value of x is often denoted Δx (or δx when this change is considered to be small.) The _____ dx represents such a change, but is infinitely small.

 a. The Method of Mechanical Theorems   b. Local maximum
 c. Dirichlet integral   d. Differential

66. A _____ is a mathematical equation for an unknown function of one or several variables that relates the values of the function itself and of its derivatives of various orders. they play a prominent role in engineering, physics, economics and other disciplines.

A simplified real world example of a _____ is modeling the acceleration of a ball falling through the air (considering only gravity and air resistance.)

 a. Structural stability   b. Caloric polynomial
 c. Differential equation   d. Phase line

67. In mathematics, the _____ Ai(x) is a special function named after the British astronomer George Biddell Airy. The function Ai(x) and the related function Bi(x), which is also called an _____, are solutions to the differential equation

$$y'' - xy = 0,$$

known as the Airy equation or the Stokes equation. This is the simplest second-order linear differential equation with a turning point (a point where the character of the solutions changes from oscillatory to exponential.)

 a. AUSM   b. ACTRAN
 c. Airy function   d. ALGOR

Chapter 11. VECTORS, CURVES, AND SURFACES IN SPACE

1. In computer science and information science, _____ could also be a method or an algorithm. Again, an example will illustrate: There are systems of counting, as with Roman numerals, and various systems for filing papers, or catalogues, and various library systems, of which the Dewey Decimal _____ is an example. This still fits with the definition of components which are connected together (in this case in order to facilitate the flow of information.)
   a. 15 theorem
   b. BIBO stability
   c. System
   d. BDDC

2. Cantor defined two kinds of _____ numbers, the ordinal numbers and the cardinal numbers. Ordinal numbers may be identified with well-ordered sets, or counting carried on to any stopping point, including points after an _____ number have already been counted. Generalizing finite and the ordinary _____ sequences which are maps from the positive integers leads to mappings from ordinal numbers, and transfinite sequences.
   a. AUSM
   b. ACTRAN
   c. Infinite
   d. ALGOR

3. The terms of the series are often produced according to a certain rule, such as by a formula, by an algorithm, by a sequence of measurements, or even by a random number generator. As there are an infinite number of terms, this notion is often called an _____. Unlike finite summations, series need tools from mathematical analysis to be fully understood and manipulated.
   a. Extreme value
   b. Integration by substitution
   c. Extreme Value Theorem
   d. Infinite Series

4. In elementary mathematics, physics, and engineering, a _____ is a geometric object that has both a magnitude (or length), direction and sense, (i.e., orientation along the given direction.) A _____ is frequently represented by a line segment with a definite direction, or graphically as an arrow, connecting an initial point A with a terminal point B, and denoted by

The magnitude of the _____ is the length of the segment and the direction characterizes the displacement of B relative to A: how much one should move the point A to 'carry' it to the point B.

Many algebraic operations on real numbers have close analogues for vectors.

   a. 15 theorem
   b. Linear partial differential operator
   c. Vector
   d. BDDC

5. In physics, _____ is defined as the rate of change of position. it is vector physical quantity; both speed and direction are required to define it. In the SI (metric) system, it is measured in meters per second: (m/s) or ms^{-1}.
   a. BIBO stability
   b. Velocity
   c. 15 theorem
   d. BDDC

6. _____ is the long dimension of any object. The _____ of a thing is the distance between its ends, its linear extent as measured from end to end. This may be distinguished from height, which is vertical extent, and width or breadth, which are the distance from side to side, measuring across the object at right angles to the _____.

a. Length
b. 15 theorem
c. BIBO stability
d. BDDC

7. In geometry, a _____ is a quadrilateral with two sets of parallel sides. The opposite or facing sides of a _____ are of equal length, and the opposite angles of a _____ are of equal size. The three-dimensional counterpart of a _____ is a parallelepiped.
   a. BDDC
   b. Parallelogram
   c. 15 theorem
   d. BIBO stability

8. _____ is how much exposed area an object has. It is expressed in square units. If an object has flat faces, its _____ can be calculated by adding together the areas of its faces.
   a. Lipschitz domain
   b. Surface area
   c. Plane curve
   d. Vector area

9. In mathematics, a _____ is an ordered list of objects (or events). Like a set, it contains members (also called elements or terms), and the number of terms (possibly infinite) is called the length of the _____. Unlike a set, order matters, and the exact same elements can appear multiple times at different positions in the _____.
   a. 15 theorem
   b. Slope
   c. Y-intercept
   d. Sequence

10. In mathematics, _____ are a concept central to linear algebra and related fields of mathematics

Suppose that K is a field and V is a vector space over K. As usual, we call elements of V vectors and call elements of K scalars.

   a. Linear combinations
   b. 15 theorem
   c. Permutation
   d. Fundamental theorem of algebra

11. In mathematics and its applications, a _____ system is a system for assigning an n-tuple of numbers or scalars to each point in an n-dimensional space. This concept is part of the theory of manifolds. 'Scalars' in many cases means real numbers, but, depending on context, can mean complex numbers or elements of some other commutative ring.
   a. Spherical coordinate system
   b. 15 theorem
   c. Cylindrical coordinate system
   d. Coordinate

12. A _____ is the curve defined by the path of a point on the edge of circular wheel as the wheel rolls along a straight line. It is an example of a roulette, a curve generated by a curve rolling on another curve.

The _____ is the solution to the brachistochrone problem (i.e. it is the curve of fastest descent under gravity) and the related tautochrone problem (i.e. the period of a ball rolling back and forth inside it does not depend on the ball's starting position.)

   a. Curtate cycloid
   b. Tractrix
   c. Prolate cycloid
   d. Cycloid

Chapter 11. VECTORS, CURVES, AND SURFACES IN SPACE

13. In differential calculus, an inflection point, or _____ (or inflexion) is a point on a curve at which the curvature changes sign. The curve changes from being concave upwards (positive curvature) to concave downwards (negative curvature), or vice versa. If one imagines driving a vehicle along the curve, it is a point at which the steering-wheel is momentarily 'straight', being turned from left to right or vice versa.
   a. Point of inflection
   b. Derivative of a constant
   c. Logarithmic derivative
   d. Lin-Tsien equation

14. A _____ is perfectly round geometrical object in three-dimensional space, such as the shape of a round ball. Like a circle in two dimensions, a perfect _____ is completely symmetrical around its center, with all points on the surface lying the same distance r from the center point. This distance r is known as the radius of the _____.
   a. Tangent line
   b. North pole
   c. Minimal surface
   d. Sphere

15. Integration is an important concept in mathematics, specifically in the field of calculus and, more broadly, mathematical analysis. Given a function f of a real variable x and an interval [a, b] of the real line, the _____

$$\int_a^b f(x)\,dx,$$

is defined informally to be the net signed area of the region in the xy-plane bounded by the graph of f, the x-axis, and the vertical lines x = a and x = b.

The term '_____' may also refer to the notion of antiderivative, a function F whose derivative is the given function f.

   a. Integrand
   b. Integral test for convergence
   c. Indefinite integral
   d. Integral

16. In infinitesimal calculus, a _____ is traditionally an infinitesimally small change in a variable. For example, if x is a variable, then a change in the value of x is often denoted Δx (or δx when this change is considered to be small.) The _____ dx represents such a change, but is infinitely small.
   a. Differential
   b. Dirichlet integral
   c. Local maximum
   d. The Method of Mechanical Theorems

17. In a totally ordered set all elements are mutually comparable, so such a set can have at most one minimal element and at most one maximal element. Then, due to mutual comparability, the minimal element will also be the least element and the maximal element will also be the greatest element. Thus in a totally ordered set we can simply use the terms minimum and _____.
   a. Racetrack principle
   b. Nth term
   c. Maximum
   d. Leibniz rule

18. In a totally ordered set all elements are mutually comparable, so such a set can have at most one minimal element and at most one maximal element. Then, due to mutual comparability, the minimal element will also be the least element and the maximal element will also be the greatest element. Thus in a totally ordered set we can simply use the terms _____ and maximum.

Chapter 11. VECTORS, CURVES, AND SURFACES IN SPACE

a. Minimum
b. Ghosts of departed quantities
c. Maximum
d. Nth term

19. In acoustics and telecommunication, a _____ of a wave is a component frequency of the signal that is an integer multiple of the fundamental frequency. For example, if the fundamental frequency is f, the harmonics have frequencies f, 2f, 3f, 4f, etc. The harmonics have the property that they are all periodic at the fundamental frequency, therefore the sum of harmonics is also periodic at that frequency.

a. 15 theorem
b. BDDC
c. BIBO stability
d. Harmonic

20. In mathematics, the _____ is the infinite series

$$\sum_{k=1}^{\infty} \frac{1}{k} = 1 + \frac{1}{2} + \frac{1}{3} + \frac{1}{4} + \cdots.$$

Its name derives from the concept of overtones, or harmonics, in music: the wavelengths of the overtones of a vibrating string are 1/2, 1/3, 1/4, etc., of the string's fundamental wavelength. Every term of the series after the first is the harmonic mean of the neighboring terms; the term harmonic mean likewise derives from music.

The _____ diverges to infinity, albeit rather slowly (the first 10^{43} terms sum to less than 100 .)

a. 15 theorem
b. BDDC
c. BIBO stability
d. Harmonic series

21. The _____ of an angle is the ratio of the length of the adjacent side to the length of the hypotenuse. In our case

$$\cos A = \frac{\text{adjacent}}{\text{hypotenuse}} = \frac{b}{h}.$$

The tangent of an angle is the ratio of the length of the opposite side to the length of the adjacent side. In our case

$$\tan A = \frac{\text{opposite}}{\text{adjacent}} = \frac{a}{b}.$$

The remaining three functions are best defined using the above three functions.

a. Sine integral
b. Trigonometric
c. Trigonometric functions
d. Cosine

22. The _____ is the derived unit of energy in the International System of Units. It is defined as:

Chapter 11. VECTORS, CURVES, AND SURFACES IN SPACE

$$1\,\text{J} = 1\,\text{kg} \cdot \text{m}^2 \cdot \text{s}^{-2}$$

One _____ is the amount of energy required to perform the following physical actions:

- The work done by a force of one newton travelling through a distance of one metre;
- The work required to move an electric charge of one coulomb through an electrical potential difference of one volt; or one coulomb volt, with the symbol CÂ·V;
- The work done to produce the power of one watt continuously for one second; or one watt second (compare kilowatt hour), with the symbol WÂ·s. Thus a kilowatt hour is 3,600,000 joules or 3.6 megajoules;

1 _____ is equal to:

- 1×10^7 ergs (exactly)
- 1.6022×10^{19} eV (electronvolts)
- 0.2390 cal (gram calories or small calories)
- 2.3901×10^{-4} kcal (kilocalories, kilogram calories, large calories or food calories)
- 9.4782×10^{-4} BTU (British thermal unit)
- 0.7376 ftÂ·lbf (foot-pound force)
- 23.7 ftÂ·pdl (foot-poundals)
- 2.7778×10^{-7} kilowatt-hour
- 2.7778×10^{-4} watt-hour
- 9.8692×10^{-3} litre-atmosphere
- 1×10^{-44} Foe (exactly)

Units defined in terms of the _____ include:

- 1 thermochemical calorie = 4.184 J
- 1 International Table calorie = 4.1868 J
- 1 watt hour = 3600 J
- 1 kilowatt hour = 3.6×10^6 J (or 3.6 MJ)
- 1 ton TNT exploding = 4.184 GJ

Useful to remember:

- 1 _____ = 1 newton × 1 meter = 1 watt × 1 second

One _____ in everyday life is approximately:

- the energy required to lift a small apple one metre straight up.
- the energy released when that same apple falls one meter to the ground.
- the energy released as heat by a quiet person, every hundredth of a second.
- the energy required to heat one gram of dry, cool air by 1 degree Celsius.
- one hundredth of the energy a person can receive by drinking a drop of beer.
- the kinetic energy of an adult human moving a distance of about a handspan every second.

- Conversion of units
- Orders of magnitude (energy)
- Fluence

a. BIBO stability
b. BDDC
c. Joule
d. 15 theorem

23. In mathematics, the _____ is a binary operation on two vectors in a three-dimensional Euclidean space that results in another vector which is perpendicular to the plane containing the two input vectors. The algebra defined by the _____ is neither commutative nor associative. It contrasts with the dot product which produces a scalar result.
a. Permutation
b. Fundamental theorem of algebra
c. 15 theorem
d. Cross product

24. In algebra, a _____ is a function depending on n that associates a scalar, det(A), to an n×n square matrix A. The fundamental geometric meaning of a _____ is a scale factor for measure when A is regarded as a linear transformation. Determinants are important both in calculus, where they enter the substitution rule for several variables, and in multilinear algebra.

For a fixed nonnegative integer n, there is a unique _____ function for the n×n matrices over any commutative ring R. In particular, this function exists when R is the field of real or complex numbers.

a. BDDC
b. 15 theorem
c. BIBO stability
d. Determinant

25. In calculus, a branch of mathematics, the _____ is a measurement of how a function changes when its input changes. Loosely speaking, a _____ can be thought of as how much a quantity is changing at some given point. For example, the _____ of the position (or distance) of a vehicle with respect to time is the instantaneous velocity (respectively, instantaneous speed) at which the vehicle is traveling.

The process of finding a _____ is called differentiation. The fundamental theorem of calculus states that differentiation is the reverse process to integration.

a. Derivative
b. Semi-differentiability
c. Stationary phase approximation
d. Bounded function

26. _____ (including exponential decay) occurs when the growth rate of a mathematical function is proportional to the function's current value. In the case of a discrete domain of definition with equal intervals it is also called geometric growth or geometric decay (the function values form a geometric progression.)

_____ is said to follow an exponential law; the simple-_____ model is known as the Malthusian growth model.

a. Oscillating
b. Inseparable differential equation
c. Exponential growth
d. Isomonodromic deformation

27. In vector calculus, there are two ways of multiplying three vectors together, to make a _____ of vectors. Three vectors defining a parallelepiped

The scalar _____ is defined as the dot product of one of the vectors with the cross product of the other two.

Geometrically, the scalar _____

$$\mathbf{a} \cdot (\mathbf{b} \times \mathbf{c})$$

is the (signed) volume of the parallelepiped defined by the three vectors given.

a. Gradient theorem
b. Green's theorem
c. Triple product
d. Divergence

28. The _____ of any solid, liquid, plasma, vacuum or theoretical object is how much three-dimensional space it occupies, often quantified numerically. One-dimensional figures (such as lines) and two-dimensional shapes (such as squares) are assigned zero _____ in the three-dimensional space. _____ is commonly presented in units such as mL or cm^3 (milliliters or cubic centimeters.)

a. Volume
b. Dirac equation
c. Klein-Gordon equation
d. Vector potential

29. In mathematics, _____ and minima, known collectively as extrema, are the largest value (maximum) or smallest value (minimum), that a function takes in a point either within a given neighbourhood (local extremum) or on the function domain in its entirety (global extremum.)

Throughout, a point refers to an input (x), while a value refers to an output (y): one distinguishing between the maximum value and the point (or points) at which it occurs.

A real-valued function f defined on the real line is said to have a local maximum point at the point x^*, if there exists some $\varepsilon > 0$, such that $f(x^*) \geq f(x)$ when $|x - x^*| < \varepsilon$.

Chapter 11. VECTORS, CURVES, AND SURFACES IN SPACE

a. Related rates
b. Maxima
c. Racetrack principle
d. Leibniz formula

30. The concept of _____ in mathematics evolved from the concept of _____ in physics. The nth _____ of a real-valued function f(x) of a real variable about a value c is

$$\mu'_n = \int_{-\infty}^{\infty} (x-c)^n f(x)\, dx.$$

It is possible to define moments for random variables in a more general fashion than moments for real values. See Moments in metric spaces.

a. Median
b. Poisson distribution
c. Geometric mean
d. Moment

31. _____ is the tendency of a force to rotate an object about an axis (or fulcrum or pivot.) Just as a force is a push or a pull, a _____ can be thought of as a twist. The symbol for _____ is τ, the Greek letter tau.

a. 15 theorem
b. BIBO stability
c. BDDC
d. Torque

32. In mathematics, the _____ are analogs of the ordinary trigonometric or circular functions. The basic _____ are the hyperbolic sine 'sinh', and the hyperbolic cosine 'cosh', from which are derived the hyperbolic tangent 'tanh', etc., in analogy to the derived trigonometric functions. The inverse _____ are the area hyperbolic sine 'arsinh' (also called 'asinh', or sometimes by the misnomer of 'arcsinh') and so on.

a. Hyperbolic functions
b. Multiplicative inverse
c. Hyperbolic cosine
d. Signum function

33. In mathematics, the _____ of a function y = f(x) is a function that, in some fashion, 'undoes' the effect of f The _____ of f is denoted f $^{-1}$. The statements y=f(x) and x=f $^{-1}$(y) are equivalent.

a. ACTRAN
b. AUSM
c. ALGOR
d. Inverse

34. In mathematics, if f is a function from A to B then an _____ for f is a function in the opposite direction, from B to A, with the property that a round trip (a composition) from A to B to A (or from B to A to B) returns each element of the initial set to itself. Thus, if an input x into the function f produces an output y, then inputting y into the _____ f^{-1} (read f inverse, not to be confused with exponentiation) produces the output x. Not every function has an inverse; those that do are called invertible.

a. Augustin-Jean Fresnel
b. Augustin Louis Cauchy
c. Aristotle
d. Inverse function

35. In mathematics, _____ are a method of defining a curve. A simple kinematical example is when one uses a time parameter to determine the position, velocity, and other information about a body in motion.

Abstractly, a relation is given in the form of an equation, and it is shown also to be the image of functions from items such as R^n.

Chapter 11. VECTORS, CURVES, AND SURFACES IN SPACE

a. Partial derivative
b. Parametric equations
c. Shift theorem
d. Critical point

36. _____ is a term in geometry and in everyday life that refers to a property in Euclidean space of two or more lines or planes, or a combination of these. The existence and properties of parallel lines are the basis of Euclid's parallel postulate. Two lines parallel would be denoted as ABC DEF.
   a. Parallelism
   b. BIBO stability
   c. 15 theorem
   d. BDDC

37. In mathematics, a (topological) _____ is defined as follows: let I be an interval of real numbers (i.e. a non-empty connected subset of $\mathbb{R}$); then a _____ γ is a continuous mapping $\gamma : I \to X$, where X is a topological space. The _____ γ is said to be simple if it is injective, i.e. if for all x, y in I, we have $\gamma(x) = \gamma(y) \implies x = y$. If I is a closed bounded interval $[a, b]$, we also allow the possibility $\gamma(a) = \gamma(b)$ (this convention makes it possible to talk about closed simple _____.)
   a. Prolate cycloid
   b. Tractrix
   c. Closed curve
   d. Curve

38. A _____ is a special kind of space curve, i.e. a smooth curve in three-space. As a mental image of a _____ one may take the spring (although the spring is not a curve, and so is technically not a _____, it does give a convenient mental picture.) A _____ is characterised by the fact that the tangent line at any point makes a constant angle with a fixed line.
   a. BIBO stability
   b. Helix
   c. 15 theorem
   d. BDDC

39. In mathematics, the concept of a '_____' is used to describe the behavior of a function as its argument or input either 'gets close' to some point, or as the argument becomes arbitrarily large; or the behavior of a sequence's elements as their index increases indefinitely. Limits are used in calculus and other branches of mathematical analysis to define derivatives and continuity.

In formulas, _____ is usually abbreviated as lim

   a. BDDC
   b. 15 theorem
   c. BIBO stability
   d. Limit

40. A _____ is a mathematical function that maps real numbers to vectors. Vector-valued functions can be defined as:

- $\mathbf{r}(t) = f(t)\hat{\mathbf{i}} + g(t)\hat{\mathbf{j}}$ or
- $\mathbf{r}(t) = f(t)\hat{\mathbf{i}} + g(t)\hat{\mathbf{j}} + h(t)\hat{\mathbf{k}}$

where f(t), g(t) and h(t) are the coordinate functions of the parameter t, and $\hat{\mathbf{i}}$, $\hat{\mathbf{j}}$, and $\hat{\mathbf{k}}$ are unit vectors. r(t) is a vector which has its tail at the origin and its head at the coordinates evaluated by the function.

The vector shown in the graph to the right is the evaluation of the function near t=19.5 (between 6π and 6.5π; i.e., somewhat more than 3 rotations.)

   a. Vector-valued function
   b. Direction vector
   c. Direction cosines
   d. Scalar multiplication

41. In geometry, the _____ (or simply the tangent) to a curve at a given point is the straight line that 'just touches' the curve at that point (in the sense explained more precisely below.) As it passes through the point of tangency, the _____ is 'going in the same direction' as the curve, and in this sense it is the best straight-line approximation to the curve at that point. The same definition applies to space curves and curves in n-dimensional Euclidean space.

   a. Tangent line
   b. North pole
   c. Lie derivative
   d. Minimal surface

42. In physics, and more specifically kinematics, _____ is the change in velocity over time. Because velocity is a vector, it can change in two ways: a change in magnitude and/or a change in direction. In one dimension, _____ is the rate at which something speeds up or slows down.

   a. ALGOR
   b. AUSM
   c. ACTRAN
   d. Acceleration

43. A _____ is the location at which two or more bones make contact. They are constructed to allow movement and provide mechanical support, and are classified structurally and functionally. Depiction of an intervertebral disk, a cartilaginous _____. Diagram of a synovial (diarthrosis) _____.

Joints are mainly classified structurally and functionally.

   a. Joint
   b. BIBO stability
   c. 15 theorem
   d. BDDC

44. If a particular point on a sphere is (arbitrarily) designated as its _____, then the corresponding antipodal point is called the south pole and the equator is the great circle that is equidistant to them. Great circles through the two poles are called lines (or meridians) of longitude, and the line connecting the two poles is called the axis of rotation. Circles on the sphere that are parallel to the equator are lines of latitude.

   a. Minimal surface
   b. Tangent line
   c. Sphere
   d. North Pole

45. In complex analysis, a mathematical discipline, a _____ of a meromorphic function is a certain type of singularity that behaves like the singularity of $\frac{1}{z^n}$ at z = 0. This means that, in particular, a _____ of the function f(z) is a point z = a such that f(z) approaches infinity uniformly as z approaches a.

Formally, suppose U is an open subset of the complex plane C, a is an element of U and f : U {a} → C is a function which is holomorphic over its domain.

Chapter 11. VECTORS, CURVES, AND SURFACES IN SPACE

    a. Lacunary function
    c. Pole
    b. Complex logarithm
    d. Bieberbach conjecture

46. _____ is the addition of a set of numbers; the result is their sum or total. An interim or present total of a _____ process is termed the running total. The 'numbers' to be summed may be natural numbers, complex numbers, matrices, or still more complicated objects.
    a. BDDC
    c. BIBO stability
    b. Summation
    d. 15 theorem

47. A _____ is the path a moving object follows through space. The object might be a projectile or a satellite, for example. It thus includes the meaning of orbit - the path of a planet, an asteroid or a comet as it travels around a central mass.
    a. Trajectory
    c. BIBO stability
    b. BDDC
    d. 15 theorem

48. For some curves there is a smallest number L that is an upper bound on the length of any polygonal approximation. If such a number exists, then the curve is said to be rectifiable and the curve is defined to have _____ L.

Let C be a curve in Euclidean (or, generally, a metric) space X = R^n, so C is the image of a continuous function f : [a, b] → X of the interval [a, b] into X.

    a. Order of integration
    c. Integration by parametric derivatives
    b. Integrand
    d. Arc length

49. The first Frenet vector $e_1(t)$ is the _____ in the same direction, defined at each regular point of γ:

$$\mathbf{e}_1(t) = \frac{\gamma'(t)}{\|\gamma'(t)\|}.$$

If t = s is the natural parameter then the tangent vector has unit length, so that the formula simplifies:

$$\mathbf{e}_1(s) = \gamma'(s).$$

The _____ determines the orientation of the curve, or the forward direction, corresponding to the increasing values of the parameter.

The normal vector, sometimes called the curvature vector, indicates the deviance of the curve from being a straight line.

It is defined as

$$\overline{\mathbf{e}_2}(t) = \gamma''(t) - \langle \gamma''(t), \mathbf{e}_1(t) \rangle \, \mathbf{e}_1(t).$$

Its normalized form, the unit normal vector, is the second Frenet vector e₂(t) and defined as

$$\mathbf{e}_2(t) = \frac{\overline{\mathbf{e}_2}(t)}{\|\overline{\mathbf{e}_2}(t)\|}.$$

The tangent and the normal vector at point t define the osculating plane at point t.

   a. Isothermal coordinates   b. Invariant differential operator
   c. ACTRAN   d. Unit tangent vector

50. In mathematics, _____ refers to any of a number of loosely related concepts in different areas of geometry. Intuitively, _____ is the amount by which a geometric object deviates from being flat, or straight in the case of a line, but this is defined in different ways depending on the context. There is a key distinction between extrinsic _____, which is defined for objects embedded in another space (usually a Euclidean space) in a way that relates to the radius of _____ of circles that touch the object, and intrinsic _____, which is defined at each point in a differential manifold.
   a. Sphere   b. Minimal surface
   c. Curvature   d. Lie derivative

51. In geometry, _____ of a curve is found at a point that is at a distance equal to the radius of curvature lying on the normal vector. It is the point at infinity if the curvature is zero. The osculating circle to the curve is centered at the _____.
   a. Dolbeault operator   b. Strophoid
   c. Kampyle of Eudoxus   d. Center of curvature

52. A surface normal to a flat surface is a vector which is perpendicular to that surface. A normal to a non-flat surface at a point P on the surface is a vector perpendicular to the tangent plane to that surface at P. The word 'normal' is also used as an adjective: a line normal to a plane, the normal component of a force, the _____, etc. The concept of normality generalizes to orthogonality.
   a. Normal line   b. Paraboloid
   c. Hyperbolic paraboloid   d. Normal vector

53. In mathematics, a _____ in a normed vector space is a vector (often a spatial vector) whose length is 1 (the unit length.) A _____ is often denoted by a lowercase letter with a superscribed caret or e;hate;, like this: $\hat{\imath}$.

In Euclidean space, the dot product of two unit vectors is simply the cosine of the angle between them.

   a. Overdetermined   b. Unit vector
   c. ACTRAN   d. ALGOR

54. A plane curve is a curve for which X is the Euclidean plane -- these are the examples first encountered -- or in some cases the projective plane. A _____ is a curve for which X is of three dimensions, usually Euclidean space; a skew curve is a _____ which lies in no plane. These definitions also apply to algebraic curves
   a. Folium of Descartes   b. Hypocycloid
   c. Curtate cycloid   d. Space curve

Chapter 11. VECTORS, CURVES, AND SURFACES IN SPACE

55. In Geometry, the _____ is an algebraic curve defined by the equation

$$x^3 + y^3 - 3axy = 0$$

It forms a loop in the first quadrant with a double point at the origin and asymptote

$$x + y + a = 0$$

It is symmetrical about y = x.

- a. Prolate cycloid
- b. Folium of Descartes
- c. Curve
- d. Cochleoid

56. A _____ is one of the most curvilinear basic geometric shapes: It has two faces, zero vertices, and zero edges. The surface formed by the points at a fixed distance from a given straight line, the axis of the _____. The solid enclosed by this surface and by two planes perpendicular to the axis is also called a _____.
- a. BDDC
- b. 15 theorem
- c. Right circular cylinder
- d. Cylinder

57. In vector calculus, the _____ is an operator that measures the magnitude of a vector field's source or sink at a given point; the _____ of a vector field is a (signed) scalar. For example, consider air as it is heated or cooled. The relevant vector field for this example is the velocity of the moving air at a point.
- a. Green's theorem
- b. Gradient theorem
- c. Divergence
- d. Triple product

58. A _____ is a surface created by rotating a curve lying on some plane (the generatrix) around a straight line (the axis of rotation) that lies on the same plane.

Examples of surfaces generated by a straight line are the cylindrical and conical surfaces. A circle that is rotated about a (coplanar) axis through the center generates a sphere.

- a. Constant of integration
- b. Surface of revolution
- c. Shell integration
- d. Riemann sum

59. An _____ is a type of quadric surface that is a higher dimensional analogue of an ellipse. The equation of a standard axis-aligned _____ body in an xyz-Cartesian coordinate system is

$$\frac{x^2}{a^2} + \frac{y^2}{b^2} + \frac{z^2}{c^2} = 1$$

where a and b are the equatorial radii (along the x and y axes) and c is the polar radius (along the z-axis), all of which are fixed positive real numbers determining the shape of the _____.

Chapter 11. VECTORS, CURVES, AND SURFACES IN SPACE

More generally, a not-necessarily-axis-aligned _____ is defined by the equation

$$\mathbf{x}^T A \mathbf{x} = 1$$

where A is a symmetric positive definite matrix and x is a vector.

a. Ellipsoid
b. ACTRAN
c. AUSM
d. ALGOR

60. In vector calculus a _____ is a vector field which is the gradient of a scalar potential. There are two closely related concepts: path independence and irrotational vector fields. Every _____ has zero curl (and is thus irrotational), and every _____ has the path independence property.

a. Divergence Theorem
b. Del
c. Conservative vector field
d. Green's theorem

61. In mathematics a _____ is a construction in vector calculus which associates a vector to every point in a (locally) Euclidean space.

Vector fields are often used in physics to model, for example, the speed and direction of a moving fluid throughout space, or the strength and direction of some force, such as the magnetic or gravitational force, as it changes from point to point.

In the rigorous mathematical treatment, (tangent) vector fields are defined on manifolds as sections of a manifold's tangent bundle.

a. Vector field
b. BDDC
c. 15 theorem
d. BIBO stability

62. The _____ is a doubly ruled surface shaped like a saddle. In a suitable coordinate system, it can be represented by the equation

$$z = \frac{x^2}{a^2} - \frac{y^2}{b^2}.$$

This is a _____ that opens up along the x-axis and down along the y-axis.

Paraboloid of revolution

With a = b an elliptic paraboloid is a paraboloid of revolution: a surface obtained by revolving a parabola around its axis.

a. Hyperbolic paraboloid
b. Torus
c. Parametric surface
d. Paraboloid

Chapter 11. VECTORS, CURVES, AND SURFACES IN SPACE

63. In mathematics, a _____ is a point in the domain of a function of two variables which is a stationary point but not a local extremum. At such a point, in general, the surface resembles a saddle that curves up in one direction, and curves down in a different direction (like a mountain pass.) In terms of contour lines, a _____ can be recognized, in general, by a contour that appears to intersect itself.

    a. Saddle point   b. 15 theorem
    c. BIBO stability   d. BDDC

64. In mathematics, a _____ is a quadric surface of special kind. There are two kinds of paraboloids: elliptic and hyperbolic. The elliptic _____ is shaped like an oval cup and can have a maximum or minimum point.

    a. Paraboloid   b. Hyperbolic paraboloid
    c. Torus   d. PDE surfaces

65. A quadratic equation with real or complex coefficients has two solutions (or roots), not necessarily distinct, which may or may not be real, given by the _____:

$$\frac{-b \pm \sqrt{b^2 - 4ac}}{2a}$$

Example discriminant signsâ– <0: $x^2+\frac{1}{2}$â– =0: $-\frac{4}{3}x^2+\frac{4}{3}x-\frac{1}{3}$â– >0: $\frac{3}{2}x^2+\frac{1}{2}x-\frac{4}{3}$

In the above formula, the expression underneath the square root sign

$$D = b^2 - 4ac,$$

is called the discriminant of the quadratic equation.

A quadratic equation with real coefficients can have either one or two distinct real roots, or two distinct complex roots. In this case the discriminant determines the number and nature of the roots.

    a. Cubic function   b. Quadratic formula
    c. Quartic function   d. Linear equation

Chapter 12. PARTIAL DIFFERENTIATION

1. _____ is a field of mathematics that deals with functionals, as opposed to ordinary calculus which deals with functions. Such functionals can for example be formed as integrals involving an unknown function and its derivatives. The interest is in extremal functions: those making the functional attain a maximum or minimum value.
    a. Hu-Washizu principle
    b. Variational vector field
    c. First variation
    d. Calculus of variations

2. In mathematics and statistics, the _____ of a list of numbers is the sum of all of the list divided by the number of items in the list. If the list is a statistical population, then the mean of that population is called a population mean. If the list is a statistical sample, we call the resulting statistic a sample mean.
    a. Arithmetic mean
    b. AUSM
    c. ACTRAN
    d. ALGOR

3. In probability theory and statistics, the _____ (or expectation value or mean and for continuous random variables with a density function it is the probability density -weighted integral of the possible values.

The term '_____' can be misleading.

    a. Expected value
    b. ALGOR
    c. AUSM
    d. ACTRAN

4. _____ is any effect, either deliberately engendered or inherent to a system, that tends to reduce the amplitude of oscillations of an oscillatory system.

In physics and engineering, _____ may be mathematically modelled as a force synchronous with the velocity of the object but opposite in direction to it. If such force is also proportional to the velocity, as for a simple mechanical viscous damper (dashpot), the force F may be related to the velocity v by

$$\mathbf{F} = -c\mathbf{v}$$

where c is the viscous _____ coefficient, given in units of newton-seconds per meter.

    a. BDDC
    b. 15 theorem
    c. BIBO stability
    d. Damping

5. In mathematics, the _____ (or replacement set) of a given function is the set of 'input' values for which the function is defined. For instance, the _____ of cosine would be all real numbers, while the _____ of the square root would be only numbers greater than or equal to 0 (ignoring complex numbers in both cases.) In a representation of a function in a xy Cartesian coordinate system, the _____ is represented on the x axis (or abscissa.)
    a. BDDC
    b. 15 theorem
    c. BIBO stability
    d. Domain

6. The _____ is the equation of state of a hypothetical ideal gas, first stated by Benoît Paul Émile Clapeyron in 1834. The law is derived from the fact that in the ideal state of any gas a given number of its 'particles' occupy the same volume, and that volume changes are inverse to pressure changes and linear to temperature changes.

Chapter 12. PARTIAL DIFFERENTIATION

The state of an amount of gas is determined by its pressure, volume, and temperature according to the equation:

$$pV = nRT$$

where

        p is the absolute pressure of the gas,
        V is the volume of the gas,
        n is the number of moles of gas,
        R is the universal gas constant,
        T is the absolute temperature.

a. Ideal gas law   b. ACTRAN
c. AUSM   d. ALGOR

7. _____ is a type of motion in which the velocity of an object changes equal amounts in equal time periods. An example of an object having _____ would be a ball rolling down a ramp. The object picks up velocity as it goes down the ramp with equal changes in time.
a. ALGOR   b. AUSM
c. Uniform Acceleration   d. ACTRAN

8. The terms '_____' and 'independent variable' are used in similar but subtly different ways in mathematics and statistics as part of the standard terminology in those subjects. They are used to distinguish between two types of quantities being considered, separating them into those available at the start of a process and those being created by it, where the latter (dependent variables) are dependent on the former (independent variables.)

In traditional calculus, a function is defined as a relation between two terms called variables because their values vary.

a. BIBO stability   b. Dependent variable
c. 15 theorem   d. BDDC

9. The terms 'dependent variable' and '_____' are used in similar but subtly different ways in mathematics and statistics as part of the standard terminology in those subjects. They are used to distinguish between two types of quantities being considered, separating them into those available at the start of a process and those being created by it, where the latter (dependent variables) are dependent on the former (independent variables.)

In traditional calculus, a function is defined as a relation between two terms called variables because their values vary.

a. ALGOR   b. ACTRAN
c. AUSM   d. Independent variable

10. The _____ of an angle is the ratio of the length of the adjacent side to the length of the hypotenuse. In our case

$$\cos A = \frac{\text{adjacent}}{\text{hypotenuse}} = \frac{b}{h}.$$

The tangent of an angle is the ratio of the length of the opposite side to the length of the adjacent side. In our case

$$\tan A = \frac{\text{opposite}}{\text{adjacent}} = \frac{a}{b}.$$

The remaining three functions are best defined using the above three functions.

- a. Cosine
- b. Trigonometric
- c. Sine integral
- d. Trigonometric functions

11. Cantor defined two kinds of _____ numbers, the ordinal numbers and the cardinal numbers. Ordinal numbers may be identified with well-ordered sets, or counting carried on to any stopping point, including points after an _____ number have already been counted. Generalizing finite and the ordinary _____ sequences which are maps from the positive integers leads to mappings from ordinal numbers, and transfinite sequences.
- a. ACTRAN
- b. ALGOR
- c. Infinite
- d. AUSM

12. When the number of variables is two, this is a _____, if it is three this is a level surface, and for higher values of n the level set is a level hypersurface.

More specifically, a _____ is the set of all real-valued roots of an equation in two variables x_1 and x_2. A level surface is the set of all real-valued roots of an equation in three variables x_1, x_2 and x_3.

- a. Scalar field
- b. Multipole moment
- c. Partial derivative
- d. Level curve

13. In mathematics, a (topological) _____ is defined as follows: let I be an interval of real numbers (i.e. a non-empty connected subset of $\mathbb{R}$); then a _____ γ is a continuous mapping $\gamma : I \to X$, where X is a topological space. The _____ γ is said to be simple if it is injective, i.e. if for all x, y in I, we have $\gamma(x) = \gamma(y) \implies x = y$. If I is a closed bounded interval $[a, b]$, we also allow the possibility $\gamma(a) = \gamma(b)$ (this convention makes it possible to talk about closed simple _____.)
- a. Prolate cycloid
- b. Curve
- c. Tractrix
- d. Closed curve

14. In mathematics, the concept of a '_____' is used to describe the behavior of a function as its argument or input either 'gets close' to some point, or as the argument becomes arbitrarily large; or the behavior of a sequence's elements as their index increases indefinitely. Limits are used in calculus and other branches of mathematical analysis to define derivatives and continuity.

Chapter 12. PARTIAL DIFFERENTIATION

In formulas, _____ is usually abbreviated as lim

a. 15 theorem
b. BDDC
c. Limit
d. BIBO stability

15. In algebra, a _____ is a function depending on n that associates a scalar, det(A), to an n×n square matrix A. The fundamental geometric meaning of a _____ is a scale factor for measure when A is regarded as a linear transformation. Determinants are important both in calculus, where they enter the substitution rule for several variables, and in multilinear algebra.

For a fixed nonnegative integer n, there is a unique _____ function for the n×n matrices over any commutative ring R. In particular, this function exists when R is the field of real or complex numbers.

a. Determinant
b. 15 theorem
c. BDDC
d. BIBO stability

16. The function difference divided by the point difference is known as the _____, it is also known as Newton's quotient):

$$\frac{\Delta F(P)}{\Delta P} = \frac{F(P + \Delta P) - F(P)}{\Delta P} = \frac{\nabla F(P + \Delta P)}{\Delta P}.$$

If ΔP is infinitesimal, then the _____ is a derivative, otherwise it is a divided difference:

$$\text{If } |\Delta P| = iota: \quad \frac{\Delta F(P)}{\Delta P} = \frac{dF(P)}{dP} = F'(P) = G(P);$$

$$\text{If } |\Delta P| > iota: \quad \frac{\Delta F(P)}{\Delta P} = \frac{DF(P)}{DP} = F[P, P + \Delta P].$$

Regardless if ΔP is infinitesimal or finite, there is (at least--in the case of the derivative--theoretically) a point range, where the boundaries are P ± (.5)ΔP (depending on the orientation--ΔF(P), δF(P) or ∇F(P)):

LB = Lower Boundary; UB = Upper Boundary;

Anyone familiar with derivatives knows that they can be regarded as functions themselves, harboring their own derivatives. Thus each function is home to sequential degrees ('higher orders') of derivation, or differentiation. This property can be generalized to all difference quotients.As this sequencing requires a corresponding boundary splintering, it is practical to break up the point range into smaller, equi-sized sections, with each section being marked by an intermediary point ('P_i'), where LB = P_0 and UB = P_{A_n}, the nth point, equaling the degree/order:

Chapter 12. PARTIAL DIFFERENTIATION

LB = $P_0 = P_0 + 0\Delta_1P = P_{A_n} - (Åf-0)\Delta_1P$; $P_1 = P_0 + 1\Delta_1P = P_{A_n} - (Åf-1)\Delta_1P$; $P_2 = P_0 + 2\Delta_1P = P_{A_n} - (Åf-2)\Delta_1P$; $P_3 = P_0 + 3\Delta_1P = P_{A_n} - (Åf-3)\Delta_1P$; ↓↓↓↓ $P_{A_n\text{-}3} = P_0 + (Åf-3)\Delta_1P = P_{A_n} - 3\Delta_1P$; $P_{A_n\text{-}2} = P_0 + (Åf-2)\Delta_1P = P_{A_n} - 2\Delta_1P$; $P_{A_n\text{-}1} = P_0 + (Åf-1)\Delta_1P = P_{A_n} - 1\Delta_1P$; UB = $P_{A_n\text{-}0} = P_0 + (Åf-0)\Delta_1P = P_{A_n} - 0\Delta_1P = P_{A_n}$;

$\Delta P = \Delta_1P = P_1 - P_0 = P_2 - P_1 = P_3 - P_2 = \ldots$

    a. Directional derivative   b. Difference quotient
    c. Notation for differentiation   d. Continuously differentiable

17. In acoustics and telecommunication, a _____ of a wave is a component frequency of the signal that is an integer multiple of the fundamental frequency. For example, if the fundamental frequency is f, the harmonics have frequencies f, 2f, 3f, 4f, etc. The harmonics have the property that they are all periodic at the fundamental frequency, therefore the sum of harmonics is also periodic at that frequency.
    a. BIBO stability   b. BDDC
    c. 15 theorem   d. Harmonic

18. In mathematics, the _____ is the infinite series

$$\sum_{k=1}^{\infty} \frac{1}{k} = 1 + \frac{1}{2} + \frac{1}{3} + \frac{1}{4} + \cdots.$$

Its name derives from the concept of overtones, or harmonics, in music: the wavelengths of the overtones of a vibrating string are 1/2, 1/3, 1/4, etc., of the string's fundamental wavelength. Every term of the series after the first is the harmonic mean of the neighboring terms; the term harmonic mean likewise derives from music.

The _____ diverges to infinity, albeit rather slowly (the first 10^{43} terms sum to less than 100 .)

    a. Harmonic series   b. BIBO stability
    c. 15 theorem   d. BDDC

19. _____ is the long dimension of any object. The _____ of a thing is the distance between its ends, its linear extent as measured from end to end. This may be distinguished from height, which is vertical extent, and width or breadth, which are the distance from side to side, measuring across the object at right angles to the _____.
    a. 15 theorem   b. BDDC
    c. BIBO stability   d. Length

20. In mathematics, an _____ space is a topological space whose dimension is n (where n is a fixed natural number.) The archetypical example is _____ Euclidean space, which describes Euclidean geometry in n dimensions.

Many familiar geometric objects can be generalized to any number of dimensions.

a. BDDC
c. 15 theorem
b. BIBO stability
d. N-dimensional

21. _____ is the change in population over time, and can be quantified as the change in the number of individuals in a population using 'per unit time' for measurement. The term _____ can technically refer to any species, but almost always refers to humans, and it is often used informally for the more specific demographic term _____ rate , and is often used to refer specifically to the growth of the population of the world.

Simple models of _____ include the Malthusian Growth Model and the logistic model.

a. Population growth
c. BIBO stability
b. BDDC
d. 15 theorem

22. In elementary mathematics, physics, and engineering, a _____ is a geometric object that has both a magnitude (or length), direction and sense, (i.e., orientation along the given direction.) A _____ is frequently represented by a line segment with a definite direction, or graphically as an arrow, connecting an initial point A with a terminal point B, and denoted by

The magnitude of the _____ is the length of the segment and the direction characterizes the displacement of B relative to A: how much one should move the point A to 'carry' it to the point B.

Many algebraic operations on real numbers have close analogues for vectors.

a. Vector
c. BDDC
b. Linear partial differential operator
d. 15 theorem

23. In mathematics, a _____ of a function of several variables is its derivative with respect to one of those variables with the others held constant (as opposed to the total derivative, in which all variables are allowed to vary.) Partial derivatives are useful in vector calculus and differential geometry.

The _____ of a function f with respect to the variable x is written as f'_x, $\partial_x f$, or $\partial f/\partial x$.

a. Jacobian
c. Level curve
b. Differentiation operator
d. Partial derivative

24. In calculus, a branch of mathematics, the _____ is a measurement of how a function changes when its input changes. Loosely speaking, a _____ can be thought of as how much a quantity is changing at some given point. For example, the _____ of the position (or distance) of a vehicle with respect to time is the instantaneous velocity (respectively, instantaneous speed) at which the vehicle is traveling.

The process of finding a _____ is called differentiation. The fundamental theorem of calculus states that differentiation is the reverse process to integration.

Chapter 12. PARTIAL DIFFERENTIATION

a. Derivative
b. Semi-differentiability
c. Stationary phase approximation
d. Bounded function

25. In geometry, the _____ (or simply the tangent) to a curve at a given point is the straight line that 'just touches' the curve at that point (in the sense explained more precisely below.) As it passes through the point of tangency, the _____ is 'going in the same direction' as the curve, and in this sense it is the best straight-line approximation to the curve at that point. The same definition applies to space curves and curves in n-dimensional Euclidean space.

a. North pole
b. Lie derivative
c. Tangent line
d. Minimal surface

26. A surface normal to a flat surface is a vector which is perpendicular to that surface. A normal to a non-flat surface at a point P on the surface is a vector perpendicular to the tangent plane to that surface at P. The word 'normal' is also used as an adjective: a line normal to a plane, the normal component of a force, the _____, etc. The concept of normality generalizes to orthogonality.

a. Hyperbolic paraboloid
b. Paraboloid
c. Normal line
d. Normal vector

27. In a totally ordered set all elements are mutually comparable, so such a set can have at most one minimal element and at most one maximal element. Then, due to mutual comparability, the minimal element will also be the least element and the maximal element will also be the greatest element. Thus in a totally ordered set we can simply use the terms minimum and _____.

a. Nth term
b. Maximum
c. Racetrack principle
d. Leibniz rule

28. In a totally ordered set all elements are mutually comparable, so such a set can have at most one minimal element and at most one maximal element. Then, due to mutual comparability, the minimal element will also be the least element and the maximal element will also be the greatest element. Thus in a totally ordered set we can simply use the terms _____ and maximum.

a. Ghosts of departed quantities
b. Minimum
c. Maximum
d. Nth term

29. In mathematics, the interior of a set S consists of all points of S that are intuitively 'not on the edge of S'. A point that is in the interior of S is an _____ of S.

The exterior of a set is the interior of its complement; it consists of the points that are not in the set or its boundary.

a. ALGOR
b. ACTRAN
c. AUSM
d. Interior point

30. A real-valued function f defined on the real line is said to have a _____ point at the point x^*, if there exists some $>\varepsilon > 0$, such that $f(x^*) \geq f(x)$ when $|x - x^*| < >\varepsilon$. The value of the function at this point is called maximum of the function.

On a graph of a function, its local maxima will look like the tops of hills.

Chapter 12. PARTIAL DIFFERENTIATION

a. Test for Divergence
b. Standard part function
c. Racetrack principle
d. Local maximum

31. In mathematics, a _____ (or critical number) is a point on the domain of a function where:

- one dimension: the derivative (or slope of the line when visualized) is equal to zero or a point where the function ceases to be differentiable.
- in general: there are two distinct concepts: either the derivative (Jacobian) vanishes, or it is not of full rank (or, in either case, the function is not differentiable); these agree in one dimension.

Note that in one dimension, a critical value or critical number x of function f is the domain element at which the derivative is zero or undefined, whereas the associated ordered pair (x, y) is the _____. In higher dimensions a critical value is in the range whereas a _____ is in the domain.

There are two situations in which a point becomes a _____ of a function of one variable. The first of which is that the value of the first derivative is equal to zero.

a. Multivariable calculus
b. Total derivative
c. Differentiation operator
d. Critical point

32. In infinitesimal calculus, a _____ is traditionally an infinitesimally small change in a variable. For example, if x is a variable, then a change in the value of x is often denoted Δx (or δx when this change is considered to be small.) The _____ dx represents such a change, but is infinitely small.

a. Local maximum
b. Dirichlet integral
c. The Method of Mechanical Theorems
d. Differential

33. In mathematics, a _____ is an approximation of a general function using a linear function (more precisely, an affine function.)

Given a differentiable function f of one real variable, Taylor's theorem for n=1 states that

$$f(x) = f(a) + f\,'(a)(x - a) + R_2$$

where R_2 is the remainder term. The _____ is obtained by dropping the remainder:

$$f(x) \approx f(a) + f\,'(a)(x - a)$$

which is true for x close to a.

a. Linear approximation
b. Smooth function
c. Lin-Tsien equation
d. Point of inflection

Chapter 12. PARTIAL DIFFERENTIATION

34. To put it differently, the class C⁰ consists of all continuous functions. The class C¹ consists of all differentiable functions whose derivative is continuous; such functions are called _____. Thus, a C¹ function is exactly a function whose derivative exists and is of class C⁰.
    a. Linear approximation
    b. Point of inflection
    c. Lin-Tsien equation
    d. Continuously differentiable

35. The _____ in some data is the discrepancy between an exact value and some approximation to it. An _____ can occur because

    1. the measurement of the data is not precise (due to the instruments), or
    2. approximations are used instead of the real data (e.g., 3.14 instead of π.)

In the mathematical field of numerical analysis, the numerical stability of an algorithm in numerical analysis indicates how the error is propagated by the algorithm.

One commonly distinguishes between the relative error and the absolute error. The absolute error is the magnitude of the difference between the exact value and the approximation.

   a. ALGOR
   b. AUSM
   c. ACTRAN
   d. Approximation error

36. f'(x) is twice the absolute value function, and it does not have a derivative at zero. Similar examples show that a function can have k derivatives for any non-negative integer k but no (k + 1)-order derivative. A function that has k successive derivatives is called _____.
    a. Power series
    b. Differential coefficient
    c. K times differentiable
    d. Differential calculus

37. In calculus, the _____ is a formula for the derivative of the composite of two functions.

In intuitive terms, if a variable, y, depends on a second variable, u, which in turn depends on a third variable, x, then the rate of change of y with respect to x can be computed as the rate of change of y with respect to u multiplied by the rate of change of u with respect to x. Schematically,

$$\frac{dy}{dx} = \frac{dy}{du} \cdot \frac{du}{dx}.$$

   a. Product rule
   b. Differentiation rules
   c. Reciprocal Rule
   d. Chain rule

38. In Geometry, the _____ is an algebraic curve defined by the equation

$$x^3 + y^3 - 3axy = 0.$$

It forms a loop in the first quadrant with a double point at the origin and asymptote

$$x + y + a = 0.$$

It is symmetrical about y = x.

- a. Curve
- b. Folium of Descartes
- c. Cochleoid
- d. Prolate cycloid

39. _____ is used to describe the steepness, incline, gradient, or grade of a straight line. A higher _____ value indicates a steeper incline. The _____ is defined as the ratio of the 'rise' divided by the 'run' between two points on a line, or in other words, the ratio of the altitude change to the horizontal distance between any two points on the line.
- a. Y-intercept
- b. Slope
- c. 15 theorem
- d. Sequence

40. A _____ is a type of manifold that is locally similar enough to Euclidean space to allow one to do calculus Any manifold can be described by a collection of charts, also known as an atlas.
- a. Tangent line
- b. Differentiable manifold
- c. Minimal surface
- d. Sphere

41. In mathematics, the _____ of a multivariate differentiable function along a given vector V at a given point P intuitively represents the instantaneous rate of change of the function, moving through P, in the direction of V. It therefore generalizes the notion of a partial derivative, in which the direction is always taken parallel to one of the coordinate axes.

The _____ is a special case of the Gâteaux derivative.

The _____ of a scalar function $f(\vec{x}) = f(x_1, x_2, \ldots, x_n)$ along a vector $\vec{v} = (v_1, \ldots, v_n)$ is the function defined by the limit

$$\nabla_{\vec{v}} f(\vec{x}) = \lim_{h \to 0} \frac{f(\vec{x} + h\vec{v}) - f(\vec{x})}{h}.$$

Sometimes authors write D_v instead of ∇_v.

- a. Linearity of differentiation
- b. Symmetrically continuous
- c. Differentiation of trigonometric functions
- d. Directional derivative

42. In calculus and other branches of mathematical analysis, an _____ is an algebraic expression obtained in the context of limits. Limits involving algebraic operations are often performed by replacing subexpressions by their limits; if the expression obtained after this substitution does not give enough information to determine the original limit, it is known as an _____. The indeterminate forms include 0^0, $0/0$, 1^∞, $\infty - \infty$, ∞/∞, $0\times\infty$, and ∞^0.
- a. ALGOR
- b. AUSM
- c. ACTRAN
- d. Indeterminate form

Chapter 12. PARTIAL DIFFERENTIATION

43. In calculus, the _____ determines whether a given critical point of a function is a maximum, a minimum, or neither.

Suppose that f is a function and we want to determine if f has a maximum or minimum at x. If f is increasing to the left of x and decreasing to the right of x, then x is a local maximum of f.

    a. First derivative test
    b. Partial sum
    c. Continuous function
    d. Test for Divergence

44. In vector calculus, the _____ of a scalar field is a vector field which points in the direction of the greatest rate of increase of the scalar field, and whose magnitude is the greatest rate of change.

A generalization of the _____ for functions on a Euclidean space which have values in another Euclidean space is the Jacobian. A further generalization for a function from one Banach space to another is the Fréchet derivative.

    a. Smooth function
    b. Gradient
    c. Lin-Tsien equation
    d. Symmetric derivative

45. In mathematics, a _____ is a method for approximating the total area underneath a curve on a graph, otherwise known as an integral. It may also be used to define the integration operation.

Consider a function $f: D \to \mathbf{R}$, where D is a subset of the real numbers $\mathbf{R}$, and let $I = [a, b]$ be a closed interval contained in D. A finite set of points $\{x_0, x_1, x_2, \ldots x_n\}$ such that $a = x_0 < x_1 < x_2 \ldots < x_n = b$ creates a partition

$$P = \{[x_0, x_1), [x_1, x_2), \ldots [x_{n-1}, x_n]\}$$

of I.

    a. Signed measure
    b. Riemann sum
    c. Solid of revolution
    d. Risch algorithm

46. In mathematical optimization, the method of Lagrange multipliers provides a strategy for finding the maximum/minimum of a function subject to constraints.

For example, consider the optimization problem

$$\text{maximize } f(x, y)$$
$$\text{subject to } g(x, y) = c.$$

We introduce a new variable (λ) called a _____, and study the Lagrange function defined by

$$\Lambda(x, y, \lambda) = f(x,y) - \lambda\Big(g(x,y) - c\Big).$$

If (x,y)≉ is a maximum for the original constrained problem, then there exists a λ such that (x,y,λ)≉ is a stationary point for the Lagrange function (stationary points are those points where the partial derivatives of Λ are zero.) However, not all stationary points yield a solution of the original problem.

a. Lagrange multiplier
c. BIBO stability
b. 15 theorem
d. BDDC

47. In algebra, the _____ of a polynomial with real or complex coefficients is a certain expression in the coefficients of the polynomial which is a symmetric polynomial in the coefficients and gives information on the nature of the roots; in particular, it is equal to zero if and only if the polynomial has a multiple root (i.e. a root with multiplicity greater than one) in the complex numbers. For example, the _____ of the quadratic polynomial

$$ax^2 + bx + c \text{ is } b^2 - 4ac.$$

The _____ of the cubic polynomial

$$ax^3 + bx^2 + cx + d \text{ is } b^2c^2 - 4ac^3 - 4b^3d - 27a^2d^2 + 18abcd.$$

a. Quadratic polynomial
c. Sheffer sequence
b. Discriminant
d. Resultant

48. Integration is an important concept in mathematics, specifically in the field of calculus and, more broadly, mathematical analysis. Given a function f of a real variable x and an interval [a, b] of the real line, the _____

$$\int_a^b f(x)\,dx,$$

is defined informally to be the net signed area of the region in the xy-plane bounded by the graph of f, the x-axis, and the vertical lines x = a and x = b.

The term '_____' may also refer to the notion of antiderivative, a function F whose derivative is the given function f.

a. Integral test for convergence
c. Integral
b. Integrand
d. Indefinite integral

Chapter 12. PARTIAL DIFFERENTIATION

49. In mathematics, a _____ is a point in the domain of a function of two variables which is a stationary point but not a local extremum. At such a point, in general, the surface resembles a saddle that curves up in one direction, and curves down in a different direction (like a mountain pass.) In terms of contour lines, a _____ can be recognized, in general, by a contour that appears to intersect itself.
   a. BDDC
   b. BIBO stability
   c. 15 theorem
   d. Saddle point

50. A _____ is perfectly round geometrical object in three-dimensional space, such as the shape of a round ball. Like a circle in two dimensions, a perfect _____ is completely symmetrical around its center, with all points on the surface lying the same distance r from the center point. This distance r is known as the radius of the _____.
   a. North pole
   b. Minimal surface
   c. Tangent line
   d. Sphere

51. The _____ of any solid, liquid, plasma, vacuum or theoretical object is how much three-dimensional space it occupies, often quantified numerically. One-dimensional figures (such as lines) and two-dimensional shapes (such as squares) are assigned zero _____ in the three-dimensional space. _____ is commonly presented in units such as mL or cm^3 (milliliters or cubic centimeters.)
   a. Vector potential
   b. Klein-Gordon equation
   c. Volume
   d. Dirac equation

52. In geometry, a _____ (pl. tori) is a surface of revolution generated by revolving a circle in three dimensional space about an axis coplanar with the circle, which does not touch the circle. Examples of tori include the surfaces of doughnuts and inner tubes.
   a. Torus
   b. Paraboloid
   c. Prolate
   d. Hyperbolic paraboloid

Chapter 13. MULTIPLE INTEGRALS

1. The _____ specifies the relationship between the two central operations of calculus, differentiation and integration.

The first part of the theorem, sometimes called the first _____, shows that an indefinite integration can be reversed by a differentiation.

The second part, sometimes called the second _____, allows one to compute the definite integral of a function by using any one of its infinitely many antiderivatives.

    a. Limits of integration
    b. Leibniz formula
    c. Fundamental theorem of calculus
    d. Periodic function

2. Just as the definite integral of a positive function of one variable represents the area of the region between the graph of the function and the x-axis, the _____ of a positive function of two variables represents the volume of the region between the surface defined by the function (on the three dimensional Cartesian plane where z = f(x,y)) and the plane which contains its domain. (Note that the same volume can be obtained via the triple integral -- the integral of a function in three variables -- of the constant function f(x, y, z) = 1 over the above-mentioned region between the surface and the plane.) If there are more variables, a multiple integral will yield hypervolumes of multi-dimensional functions.

    a. Constant of integration
    b. Double integral
    c. Trigonometric substitution
    d. Risch algorithm

3. In acoustics and telecommunication, a _____ of a wave is a component frequency of the signal that is an integer multiple of the fundamental frequency. For example, if the fundamental frequency is f, the harmonics have frequencies f, 2f, 3f, 4f, etc. The harmonics have the property that they are all periodic at the fundamental frequency, therefore the sum of harmonics is also periodic at that frequency.

    a. 15 theorem
    b. Harmonic
    c. BDDC
    d. BIBO stability

4. In mathematics, the _____ is the infinite series

$$\sum_{k=1}^{\infty} \frac{1}{k} = 1 + \frac{1}{2} + \frac{1}{3} + \frac{1}{4} + \cdots.$$

Its name derives from the concept of overtones, or harmonics, in music: the wavelengths of the overtones of a vibrating string are 1/2, 1/3, 1/4, etc., of the string's fundamental wavelength. Every term of the series after the first is the harmonic mean of the neighboring terms; the term harmonic mean likewise derives from music.

The _____ diverges to infinity, albeit rather slowly (the first 10^{43} terms sum to less than 100 .)

    a. Harmonic series
    b. BDDC
    c. BIBO stability
    d. 15 theorem

5. _____ is the long dimension of any object. The _____ of a thing is the distance between its ends, its linear extent as measured from end to end. This may be distinguished from height, which is vertical extent, and width or breadth, which are the distance from side to side, measuring across the object at right angles to the _____.

a. 15 theorem
b. Length
c. BDDC
d. BIBO stability

6. The _____ is a type of definite integral extended to functions of more than one real variable, for example, f(x, y) or f(x, y, z.)

Introduction

Just as the definite integral of a positive function of one variable represents the area of the region between the graph of the function and the x-axis, the double integral of a positive function of two variables represents the volume of the region between the surface defined by the function (on the three dimensional Cartesian plane where z = f(x,y)) and the plane which contains its domain. (Note that the same volume can be obtained via the triple integral -- the integral of a function in three variables -- of the constant function f(x, y, z) = 1 over the above-mentioned region between the surface and the plane.)

a. Risch algorithm
b. Multiple integral
c. Surface of revolution
d. Quadratic integral

7. In mathematics, a _____ is a method for approximating the total area underneath a curve on a graph, otherwise known as an integral. It may also be used to define the integration operation.

Consider a function f: D >→ R, where D is a subset of the real numbers R, and let I = [a, b] be a closed interval contained in D. A finite set of points $\{x_0, x_1, x_2, ... x_n\}$ such that $a = x_0 < x_1 < x_2 ... < x_n = b$ creates a partition

$$P = \{[x_0, x_1), [x_1, x_2), ... [x_{n-1}, x_n]\}$$

of I.

a. Solid of revolution
b. Signed measure
c. Risch algorithm
d. Riemann sum

8. Integration is an important concept in mathematics, specifically in the field of calculus and, more broadly, mathematical analysis. Given a function f of a real variable x and an interval [a, b] of the real line, the _____

$$\int_a^b f(x)\,dx,$$

is defined informally to be the net signed area of the region in the xy-plane bounded by the graph of f, the x-axis, and the vertical lines x = a and x = b.

The term '_____' may also refer to the notion of antiderivative, a function F whose derivative is the given function f.

a. Integral
b. Indefinite integral
c. Integral test for convergence
d. Integrand

9. In mathematics, a function f defined on some set X with real or complex values is a _____ function, if the set of its values is _____. In other words, there exists a number M>0 such that

$$|f(x)| \leq M$$

for all x in X.

Sometimes, if $f(x) \leq A$ for all x in X, then the function is said to be _____ above by A.

a. Bounded
b. Stationary phase approximation
c. Differential coefficient
d. Concave upwards

10. In geometry, a _____ (pl. tori) is a surface of revolution generated by revolving a circle in three dimensional space about an axis coplanar with the circle, which does not touch the circle. Examples of tori include the surfaces of doughnuts and inner tubes.

a. Prolate
b. Hyperbolic paraboloid
c. Paraboloid
d. Torus

11. In mathematics, an _____ is a function whose integral exists. Unless specifically stated, the integral in question is usually the Lebesgue integral. Otherwise, one can say that the function is 'Riemann-integrable' (i.e., its Riemann integral exists), 'Henstock-Kurzweil-integrable,' etc.

a. Integrable function
b. ALGOR
c. ACTRAN
d. AUSM

12. In mathematics, the concept of a '_____' is used to describe the behavior of a function as its argument or input either 'gets close' to some point, or as the argument becomes arbitrarily large; or the behavior of a sequence's elements as their index increases indefinitely. Limits are used in calculus and other branches of mathematical analysis to define derivatives and continuity.

In formulas, _____ is usually abbreviated as lim

a. 15 theorem
b. BIBO stability
c. BDDC
d. Limit

13. In calculus, interchange of the _____ is a methodology that transforms multiple integrations of functions into other, hopefully simpler, integrals by changing the order in which the integrations are performed.

Chapter 13. MULTIPLE INTEGRALS

The problem for examination is evaluation of an integral of the form:

$$\iint_D dxdy\ f(x,y),$$

where D is some two-dimensional area in the xy-plane. For some functions f straightforward integration is feasible, but where that is not true, the integral can sometimes be reduced to simpler form by changing the _____.

a. Arc length
b. Indefinite integral
c. Integration by parts
d. Order of integration

14. The _____ of any solid, liquid, plasma, vacuum or theoretical object is how much three-dimensional space it occupies, often quantified numerically. One-dimensional figures (such as lines) and two-dimensional shapes (such as squares) are assigned zero _____ in the three-dimensional space. _____ is commonly presented in units such as mL or cm³ (milliliters or cubic centimeters.)

a. Vector potential
b. Dirac equation
c. Klein-Gordon equation
d. Volume

15. To put it differently, the class C^0 consists of all continuous functions. The class C^1 consists of all differentiable functions whose derivative is continuous; such functions are called _____. Thus, a C^1 function is exactly a function whose derivative exists and is of class C^0.

a. Point of inflection
b. Linear approximation
c. Lin-Tsien equation
d. Continuously differentiable

16. In calculus, a branch of mathematics, the _____ is a measurement of how a function changes when its input changes. Loosely speaking, a _____ can be thought of as how much a quantity is changing at some given point. For example, the _____ of the position (or distance) of a vehicle with respect to time is the instantaneous velocity (respectively, instantaneous speed) at which the vehicle is traveling.

The process of finding a _____ is called differentiation. The fundamental theorem of calculus states that differentiation is the reverse process to integration.

a. Stationary phase approximation
b. Bounded function
c. Semi-differentiability
d. Derivative

17. In geometry, the _____, geometric center, or barycenter of a plane figure X is the intersection of all straight lines that divide X into two parts of equal moment about the line. Informally, it is the 'average' of all points of X. The definition extends to any object X in n-dimensional space: its _____ is the intersection of all hyperplanes that divide X into two parts of equal moment.

a. Centroid
b. BDDC
c. BIBO stability
d. 15 theorem

Chapter 13. MULTIPLE INTEGRALS

18. _____ generally conveys two primary meanings. The first is an imprecise sense of harmonious or aesthetically-pleasing proportionality and balance; such that it reflects beauty or perfection. The second meaning is a precise and well-defined concept of balance or 'patterned self-similarity' that can be demonstrated or proved according to the rules of a formal system: by geometry, through physics or otherwise.
  a. BDDC
  b. 15 theorem
  c. BIBO stability
  d. Symmetry

19. The concept of _____ in mathematics evolved from the concept of _____ in physics. The nth _____ of a real-valued function f(x) of a real variable about a value c is

$$\mu'_n = \int_{-\infty}^{\infty} (x-c)^n f(x)\, dx.$$

It is possible to define moments for random variables in a more general fashion than moments for real values. See Moments in metric spaces.

  a. Median
  b. Geometric mean
  c. Moment
  d. Poisson distribution

20. _____, also called mass _____ or the angular mass, (SI units kg m^2) is a measure of an object's resistance to changes in its rotation rate. It is the rotational analog of mass. That is, it is the inertia of a rigid rotating body with respect to its rotation.
  a. Moment of inertia
  b. Wave equation
  c. Dirac equation
  d. Klein-Gordon equation

21. _____ is a quantity used to predict an object's ability to resist torsion, in objects (or segments of objects) with an invariant circular cross-section and no significant warping or out-of-plane deformation. It is used to calculate the angular displacement of an object subjected to a torque. It is analogous to the area moment of inertia, which characterizes an object's ability to resist bending and is required to calculate displacement.
  a. Spring equation
  b. Navier-Stokes equations
  c. Polar moment of inertia
  d. Spring constant

22. _____ is the name of several related measures of the size of an object, a surface, or an ensemble of points. It is calculated as the root mean square distance of the objects' parts from either its center of gravity or an axis.

In structural engineering, the two-dimensional _____ is used to describe the distribution of cross sectional area in a beam around its centroidal axis.

  a. BDDC
  b. BIBO stability
  c. 15 theorem
  d. Radius of gyration

23. In mathematics, a _____ is a quadric surface of special kind. There are two kinds of paraboloids: elliptic and hyperbolic. The elliptic _____ is shaped like an oval cup and can have a maximum or minimum point.
  a. Torus
  b. Hyperbolic paraboloid
  c. PDE surfaces
  d. Paraboloid

Chapter 13. MULTIPLE INTEGRALS

24. Smooth functions with given closed support are used in the construction of smooth partitions of unity ; these are essential in the study of smooth manifolds, for example to show that Riemannian metrics can be defined globally starting from their local existence. A simple case is that of a bump function on the real line, that is, a _____ f that takes the value 0 outside an interval [a,b] and such that

   f(x) > 0 for a < x < b.

Given a number of overlapping intervals on the line, bump functions can be constructed on each of them, and on semi-infinite intervals (->∞, c] and [d,+>∞) to cover the whole line, such that the sum of the functions is always 1.

   a. Smooth function   b. Symmetric derivative
   c. Gradient   d. Continuously differentiable

25. In mathematics and its applications, a _____ system is a system for assigning an n-tuple of numbers or scalars to each point in an n-dimensional space. This concept is part of the theory of manifolds. 'Scalars' in many cases means real numbers, but, depending on context, can mean complex numbers or elements of some other commutative ring.

   a. 15 theorem   b. Spherical coordinate system
   c. Cylindrical coordinate system   d. Coordinate

26. A _____ is one of the most curvilinear basic geometric shapes:It has two faces, zero vertices, and zero edges. The surface formed by the points at a fixed distance from a given straight line, the axis of the _____. The solid enclosed by this surface and by two planes perpendicular to the axis is also called a _____.

   a. BDDC   b. Right circular cylinder
   c. 15 theorem   d. Cylinder

27. If a particular point on a sphere is (arbitrarily) designated as its _____, then the corresponding antipodal point is called the south pole and the equator is the great circle that is equidistant to them. Great circles through the two poles are called lines (or meridians) of longitude, and the line connecting the two poles is called the axis of rotation. Circles on the sphere that are parallel to the equator are lines of latitude.

   a. North pole   b. Tangent line
   c. Sphere   d. Minimal surface

28. A _____ is a surface in the Euclidean space R^3 which is defined by a parametric equation with two parameters. Parametric representation is the most general way to specify a surface. Surfaces that occur in two of the main theorems of vector calculus, Stokes' theorem and divergence theorem, are frequently given in a parametric form.

   a. Parametric surface   b. Torus
   c. Prolate   d. Paraboloid

29. _____ is how much exposed area an object has. It is expressed in square units. If an object has flat faces, its _____ can be calculated by adding together the areas of its faces.

   a. Vector area   b. Surface area
   c. Lipschitz domain   d. Plane curve

Chapter 13. MULTIPLE INTEGRALS

30. In mathematics, a _____ is a point in the domain of a function of two variables which is a stationary point but not a local extremum. At such a point, in general, the surface resembles a saddle that curves up in one direction, and curves down in a different direction (like a mountain pass.) In terms of contour lines, a _____ can be recognized, in general, by a contour that appears to intersect itself.
   a. BDDC
   b. BIBO stability
   c. 15 theorem
   d. Saddle point

31. _____ is used to describe the steepness, incline, gradient, or grade of a straight line. A higher _____ value indicates a steeper incline. The _____ is defined as the ratio of the 'rise' divided by the 'run' between two points on a line, or in other words, the ratio of the altitude change to the horizontal distance between any two points on the line.
   a. Y-intercept
   b. 15 theorem
   c. Sequence
   d. Slope

32. In mathematics, a (topological) _____ is defined as follows: let I be an interval of real numbers (i.e. a non-empty connected subset of $\mathbb{R}$); then a _____ γ is a continuous mapping $\gamma : I \rightarrow X$, where X is a topological space. The _____ γ is said to be simple if it is injective, i.e. if for all x, y in I, we have $\gamma(x) = \gamma(y) \implies x = y$. If I is a closed bounded interval $[a, b]$, we also allow the possibility $\gamma(a) = \gamma(b)$ (this convention makes it possible to talk about closed simple _____.)
   a. Closed curve
   b. Tractrix
   c. Curve
   d. Prolate cycloid

33. In infinitesimal calculus, a _____ is traditionally an infinitesimally small change in a variable. For example, if x is a variable, then a change in the value of x is often denoted Δx (or δx when this change is considered to be small.) The _____ dx represents such a change, but is infinitely small.
   a. The Method of Mechanical Theorems
   b. Differential
   c. Local maximum
   d. Dirichlet integral

34. A _____ is a mathematical equation for an unknown function of one or several variables that relates the values of the function itself and of its derivatives of various orders. they play a prominent role in engineering, physics, economics and other disciplines.

A simplified real world example of a _____ is modeling the acceleration of a ball falling through the air (considering only gravity and air resistance.)

   a. Phase line
   b. Structural stability
   c. Caloric polynomial
   d. Differential equation

35. In mathematics, the _____ of a function y = f(x) is a function that, in some fashion, 'undoes' the effect of f The _____ of f is denoted f^{-1}. The statements y=f(x) and x=f^{-1}(y) are equivalent.
   a. ALGOR
   b. ACTRAN
   c. AUSM
   d. Inverse

36. An injective function is called an injection, and is also said to be a _____ function (not to be confused with _____ correspondence, i.e. a bijective function.)

Chapter 13. MULTIPLE INTEGRALS

A function f that is not injective is sometimes called many-to-one. (However, this terminology is also sometimes used to mean 'single-valued', i.e. each argument is mapped to at most one value.)

a. One-to-one function
b. Injective function
c. Onto
d. One-to-one

37. In mathematics, a _____ is an ordered list of objects (or events). Like a set, it contains members (also called elements or terms), and the number of terms (possibly infinite) is called the length of the _____. Unlike a set, order matters, and the exact same elements can appear multiple times at different positions in the _____.

a. Slope
b. Sequence
c. 15 theorem
d. Y-intercept

38. In vector calculus, the _____ is shorthand for either the _____ matrix or its determinant, the _____ determinant.

In algebraic geometry the _____ of a curve means the _____ variety: a group variety associated to the curve, in which the curve can be embedded.

These concepts are all named after the mathematician Carl Gustav Jacob Jacobi.

a. Critical point
b. Vector Laplacian
c. Saddle surface
d. Jacobian

39. A _____ is a 2D geometric symbolic representation of information according to some visualization technique. Sometimes, the technique uses a 3D visualization which is then projected onto the 2D surface.

_____ has two meanings in common sense.

a. BDDC
b. BIBO stability
c. 15 theorem
d. Diagram

Chapter 14. VECTOR CALCULUS

1. In vector calculus, the _____ is an operator that measures the magnitude of a vector field's source or sink at a given point; the _____ of a vector field is a (signed) scalar. For example, consider air as it is heated or cooled. The relevant vector field for this example is the velocity of the moving air at a point.

    a. Divergence   b. Green's theorem
    c. Gradient theorem   d. Triple product

2. In vector calculus, the _____ Ostrogradskye;s theorem the _____ states that the outward flux of a vector field through a surface is equal to the triple integral of the divergence on the region inside the surface. Intuitively, it states that the sum of all sources minus the sum of all sinks gives the net flow out of a region.

    a. Divergence theorem   b. Divergence
    c. Del   d. Green's theorem

3. The method of _____ or ordinary _____ is used to solve overdetermined systems. _____ is often applied in statistical contexts, particularly regression analysis.

_____ can be interpreted as a method of fitting data. The best fit in the _____ sense is that instance of the model for which the sum of squared residuals has its least value, a residual being the difference between an observed value and the value given by the model.

    a. BDDC   b. 15 theorem
    c. BIBO stability   d. Least squares

4. In physics, the _____ or more accurately principle of stationary action is a variational principle which, when applied to the action of a mechanical system, can be used to obtain the equations of motion for that system. The principle led to the development of the Lagrangian and Hamiltonian formulations of classical mechanics.

The principle remains central in modern physics and mathematics, being applied in the theory of relativity, quantum mechanics and quantum field theory, and a focus of modern mathematical investigation in Morse theory.

    a. Maupertuis' principle   b. Principle of least action
    c. Morse-Palais lemma   d. Signorini problem

5. In elementary mathematics, physics, and engineering, a _____ is a geometric object that has both a magnitude (or length), direction and sense, (i.e., orientation along the given direction.) A _____ is frequently represented by a line segment with a definite direction, or graphically as an arrow, connecting an initial point A with a terminal point B, and denoted by

The magnitude of the _____ is the length of the segment and the direction characterizes the displacement of B relative to A: how much one should move the point A to 'carry' it to the point B.

Many algebraic operations on real numbers have close analogues for vectors.

a. 15 theorem
c. Linear partial differential operator
b. BDDC
d. Vector

6. In mathematics a _____ is a construction in vector calculus which associates a vector to every point in a (locally) Euclidean space.

Vector fields are often used in physics to model, for example, the speed and direction of a moving fluid throughout space, or the strength and direction of some force, such as the magnetic or gravitational force, as it changes from point to point.

In the rigorous mathematical treatment, (tangent) vector fields are defined on manifolds as sections of a manifold's tangent bundle.

a. BDDC
c. BIBO stability
b. 15 theorem
d. Vector field

7. In physics, _____ is defined as the rate of change of position. it is vector physical quantity; both speed and direction are required to define it. In the SI (metric) system, it is measured in meters per second: (m/s) or ms^{-1}.

a. BIBO stability
c. BDDC
b. Velocity
d. 15 theorem

8. A _____, sometimes known as an energy shield, force shield typically made of energy or charged particles, that protects a person, area or object from attacks or intrusions.

A University of Washington in Seattle group has been experimenting with using a bubble of charged plasma to surround a spacecraft, contained by a fine mesh of superconducting wire. This would protect the spacecraft from interstellar radiation and some particles without needing physical shielding.

a. 15 theorem
c. Force field
b. BIBO stability
d. BDDC

9. In vector calculus, the _____ of a scalar field is a vector field which points in the direction of the greatest rate of increase of the scalar field, and whose magnitude is the greatest rate of change.

A generalization of the _____ for functions on a Euclidean space which have values in another Euclidean space is the Jacobian. A further generalization for a function from one Banach space to another is the Fréchet derivative.

a. Gradient
c. Symmetric derivative
b. Lin-Tsien equation
d. Smooth function

10. A _____ is a type of manifold that is locally similar enough to Euclidean space to allow one to do calculus Any manifold can be described by a collection of charts, also known as an atlas.

a. Minimal surface
c. Tangent line

b. Sphere
d. Differentiable manifold

11. In mathematics, a (topological) _____ is defined as follows: let I be an interval of real numbers (i.e. a non-empty connected subset of $\mathbb{R}$); then a _____ γ is a continuous mapping $\gamma : I \to X$, where X is a topological space. The _____ γ is said to be simple if it is injective, i.e. if for all x, y in I, we have $\gamma(x) = \gamma(y) \implies x = y$. If I is a closed bounded interval $[a, b]$, we also allow the possibility $\gamma(a) = \gamma(b)$ (this convention makes it possible to talk about closed simple _____.)

a. Closed curve
c. Prolate cycloid

b. Curve
d. Tractrix

12. In infinitesimal calculus, a _____ is traditionally an infinitesimally small change in a variable. For example, if x is a variable, then a change in the value of x is often denoted Δx (or δx when this change is considered to be small.) The _____ dx represents such a change, but is infinitely small.

a. The Method of Mechanical Theorems
c. Dirichlet integral

b. Local maximum
d. Differential

13. In mathematics, a _____ is an operator defined as a function of the differentiation operator. It is helpful, as a matter of notation first, to consider differentiation as an abstract operation, accepting a function and returning another (in the style of a higher-order function in computer science.)

There are certainly reasons not to restrict to linear operators; for instance the Schwarzian derivative is a well-known non-linear operator.

a. Critical point
c. Parametric equations

b. Surface integral
d. Differential operator

14. In calculus, the _____ is a formula used to find the derivatives of products of functions. It may be stated thus:

$$(f \cdot g)' = f' \cdot g + f \cdot g'$$

or in the Leibniz notation thus:

$$\frac{d}{dx}(u \cdot v) = u \cdot \frac{dv}{dx} + v \cdot \frac{du}{dx}.$$

Discovery of this rule is credited to Gottfried Leibniz, who demonstrated it using differentials. Here is Leibniz's argument: Let u and v be two differentiable functions of x.

a. Differentiation rules
c. Product rule

b. Constant factor rule in differentiation
d. Quotient Rule

15. The _____ is a function in mathematics. The application of this function to a value x is written as exp(x). Equivalently, this can be written in the form e^x, where e is a mathematical constant, the base of the natural logarithm, which equals approximately 2.718281828, and is also known as Euler's number.

    a. Area hyperbolic functions   b. ACTRAN
    c. Integral part   d. Exponential function

16. For some curves there is a smallest number L that is an upper bound on the length of any polygonal approximation. If such a number exists, then the curve is said to be rectifiable and the curve is defined to have _____ L.

Let C be a curve in Euclidean (or, generally, a metric) space $X = R^n$, so C is the image of a continuous function $f : [a, b] \to X$ of the interval [a, b] into X.

    a. Integration by parametric derivatives   b. Integrand
    c. Order of integration   d. Arc length

17. _____ is the long dimension of any object. The _____ of a thing is the distance between its ends, its linear extent as measured from end to end. This may be distinguished from height, which is vertical extent, and width or breadth, which are the distance from side to side, measuring across the object at right angles to the _____.

    a. BIBO stability   b. 15 theorem
    c. BDDC   d. Length

18. The concept of _____ in mathematics evolved from the concept of _____ in physics. The nth _____ of a real-valued function f(x) of a real variable about a value c is

$$\mu'_n = \int_{-\infty}^{\infty} (x-c)^n f(x)\, dx.$$

It is possible to define moments for random variables in a more general fashion than moments for real values. See Moments in metric spaces.

    a. Poisson distribution   b. Median
    c. Geometric mean   d. Moment

19. _____, also called mass _____ or the angular mass, (SI units kg m^2) is a measure of an object's resistance to changes in its rotation rate. It is the rotational analog of mass. That is, it is the inertia of a rigid rotating body with respect to its rotation.

    a. Wave equation   b. Dirac equation
    c. Klein-Gordon equation   d. Moment of inertia

20. In the mathematical fields of differential geometry and tensor calculus, differential forms are an approach to multivariable calculus that is independent of coordinates. A _____ of degree k, or (differential) k-form, on a smooth manifold M is a smooth section of the kth exterior power of the cotangent bundle of M. The set of all k-forms on M is a vector space commonly denoted $\Omega^k(M).$

Chapter 14. VECTOR CALCULUS

A differential 0-form is by definition a smooth function on M. A differential 1-form is an object dual to a vector field on M.

a. Differential form
b. Hodge dual
c. Two-form
d. Soldering

21. In mathematics and its applications, a _____ system is a system for assigning an n-tuple of numbers or scalars to each point in an n-dimensional space. This concept is part of the theory of manifolds. 'Scalars' in many cases means real numbers, but, depending on context, can mean complex numbers or elements of some other commutative ring.
a. Cylindrical coordinate system
b. Spherical coordinate system
c. 15 theorem
d. Coordinate

22. In mathematics, even functions and odd functions are functions which satisfy particular symmetry relations, with respect to taking additive inverses. They are important in many areas of mathematical analysis, especially the theory of power series and Fourier series. They are named for the parity of the powers of the power functions which satisfy each condition: the function $f(x) = x^n$ is an even function if n is an even integer, and it is an _____ if n is an odd integer.
a. Even function
b. Integration by substitution
c. Integral of secant cubed
d. Odd function

23. In mathematics, an _____ on a real vector space is a choice of which ordered bases are 'positively' oriented and which are 'negatively' oriented. In the three-dimensional Euclidean space, the two possible basis orientations are called right-handed and left-handed (or right-chiral and left-chiral), respectively. However, the choice of _____ is independent of the handedness or chirality of the bases (although right-handed bases are typically declared to be positively oriented, they may also be assigned a negative _____.)
a. ALGOR
b. Unit vector
c. ACTRAN
d. Orientation

24. In mathematics, a _____ is a function whose definition is dependent on the value of the independent variable. Mathematically, a real-valued function f of a real variable x is a relationship whose definition is given differently on disjoint subsets of its domain

The word piecewise is also used to describe any property of a _____ that holds for each piece but may not hold for the whole domain of the function.

a. Surjective
b. Range
c. Piecewise-defined function
d. Constant function

25. A _____ of a curve is a line that (locally) intersects two points on the curve. The word secant comes from the Latin secare, for to cut.

It can be used to approximate the tangent to a curve, at some point P. If the secant to a curve is defined by two points, P and Q, with P fixed and Q variable, as Q approaches P along the curve, the direction of the secant approaches that of the tangent at P, assuming there is just one.

a. Kappa curve
b. Curve
c. Witch of Agnesi
d. Secant line

26. Let *f* be a differentiable function, and let f'(x) be its derivative. The derivative of f'(x) (if it has one) is written f''(x) and is called the _____ of *f*. Similarly, the derivative of a _____, if it exists, is written f'''(x) and is called the third derivative of *f*.

   a. Second derivative
   b. Stationary phase approximation
   c. Vertical asymptote
   d. Slant asymptote

27. In calculus, a branch of mathematics, the _____ is a criterion often useful for determining whether a given stationary point of a function is a local maximum or a local minimum.

The test states: If the function f is twice differentiable at a stationary point x, meaning that $f'(x) = 0$, then:

- If $f''(x) < 0$ then f has a local maximum at x.
- If $f''(x) > 0$ then f has a local minimum at x.
- If $f''(x) = 0$, the _____ says nothing about the point x, has a possible inflection point.

In the last case, the function may have a local maximum or minimum there, but the function is sufficiently 'flat' that this is undetected by the second derivative. In this case one has to examine the third derivative. Such an example is f(x) = x^4.

   a. Symmetric derivative
   b. Second derivative test
   c. Stationary point
   d. Linearity of differentiation

28. In calculus, a branch of mathematics, the _____ is a measurement of how a function changes when its input changes. Loosely speaking, a _____ can be thought of as how much a quantity is changing at some given point. For example, the _____ of the position (or distance) of a vehicle with respect to time is the instantaneous velocity (respectively, instantaneous speed) at which the vehicle is traveling.

The process of finding a _____ is called differentiation. The fundamental theorem of calculus states that differentiation is the reverse process to integration.

   a. Semi-differentiability
   b. Derivative
   c. Bounded function
   d. Stationary phase approximation

29. Integration is an important concept in mathematics, specifically in the field of calculus and, more broadly, mathematical analysis. Given a function *f* of a real variable x and an interval [a, b] of the real line, the _____

$$\int_a^b f(x)\,dx,$$

is defined informally to be the net signed area of the region in the xy-plane bounded by the graph of f, the x-axis, and the vertical lines x = a and x = b.

The term '_____' may also refer to the notion of antiderivative, a function F whose derivative is the given function f.

a. Integrand
b. Integral test for convergence
c. Indefinite integral
d. Integral

30. In mathematics, a _____ is an integral where the function to be integrated is evaluated along a curve. Various different line integrals are in use. A specific case of an integration along a closed curve in two dimensions or the complex plane is the contour integral.

a. Mittag-Leffler star
b. Radius of convergence
c. Picard theorem
d. Line integral

31. The first Frenet vector $e_1(t)$ is the _____ in the same direction, defined at each regular point of γ:

$$\mathbf{e}_1(t) = \frac{\gamma'(t)}{\|\gamma'(t)\|}.$$

If t = s is the natural parameter then the tangent vector has unit length, so that the formula simplifies:

$$\mathbf{e}_1(s) = \gamma'(s).$$

The _____ determines the orientation of the curve, or the forward direction, corresponding to the increasing values of the parameter.

The normal vector, sometimes called the curvature vector, indicates the deviance of the curve from being a straight line.

It is defined as

$$\overline{\mathbf{e}_2}(t) = \gamma''(t) - \langle \gamma''(t), \mathbf{e}_1(t) \rangle \, \mathbf{e}_1(t).$$

Its normalized form, the unit normal vector, is the second Frenet vector $e_2(t)$ and defined as

$$\mathbf{e}_2(t) = \frac{\overline{\mathbf{e}_2}(t)}{\|\overline{\mathbf{e}_2}(t)\|}.$$

The tangent and the normal vector at point t define the osculating plane at point t.

a. Invariant differential operator
b. Isothermal coordinates
c. ACTRAN
d. Unit tangent vector

32. In geometry, the _____ (or simply the tangent) to a curve at a given point is the straight line that 'just touches' the curve at that point (in the sense explained more precisely below.) As it passes through the point of tangency, the _____ is 'going in the same direction' as the curve, and in this sense it is the best straight-line approximation to the curve at that point. The same definition applies to space curves and curves in n-dimensional Euclidean space.
   a. Lie derivative
   b. North pole
   c. Minimal surface
   d. Tangent line

33. The _____ specifies the relationship between the two central operations of calculus, differentiation and integration.

The first part of the theorem, sometimes called the first _____, shows that an indefinite integration can be reversed by a differentiation.

The second part, sometimes called the second _____, allows one to compute the definite integral of a function by using any one of its infinitely many antiderivatives.

   a. Periodic function
   b. Limits of integration
   c. Leibniz formula
   d. Fundamental theorem of calculus

34. In vector calculus a _____ is a vector field which is the gradient of a scalar potential. There are two closely related concepts: path independence and irrotational vector fields. Every _____ has zero curl (and is thus irrotational), and every _____ has the path independence property.
   a. Del
   b. Conservative vector field
   c. Green's theorem
   d. Divergence Theorem

35. _____ can be thought of as energy stored within a physical system. It is called _____ because it has the potential to be converted into other forms of energy, such as kinetic energy, and to do work in the process. The standard (SI) unit of measure for _____ is the joule, the same as for work or energy in general.
   a. Potential energy
   b. BDDC
   c. 15 theorem
   d. Law of Conservation of Energy

36. In the various subfields of physics, there exist two common usages of the term _____, both with rigorous mathematical frameworks.

- In the study of transport phenomena (heat transfer, mass transfer and fluid dynamics), _____ is defined as the amount that flows through a unit area per unit time. _____ in this definition is a vector.
- In the field of electromagnetism and mathematics, _____ is usually the integral of a vector quantity over a finite surface. The result of this integration is a scalar quantity. The magnetic _____ is thus the integral of the magnetic vector field B over a surface, and the electric _____ is defined similarly. Using this definition, the _____ of the Poynting vector over a specified surface is the rate at which electromagnetic energy flows through that surface. Confusingly, the Poynting vector is sometimes called the power _____, which is an example of the first usage of _____, above. It has units of watts per square metre (W·m^{-2})

Chapter 14. VECTOR CALCULUS

One could argue, based on the work of James Clerk Maxwell, that the transport definition precedes the more recent way the term is used in electromagnetism. The specific quote from Maxwell is 'In the case of fluxes, we have to take the integral, over a surface, of the _____ through every element of the surface. The result of this operation is called the surface integral of the _____.

a. 15 theorem
b. BIBO stability
c. Flux
d. BDDC

37. In mathematics, a series (or sometimes also an integral) is said to converge absolutely if the sum (or integral) of the absolute value of the summand or integrand is finite.

More precisely, a real or complex-valued series $\sum_{n=0}^{\infty} a_n$ is said to converge absolutely if $\sum_{n=0}^{\infty} |a_n| < \infty$.

_____ is vitally important to the study of infinite series because on the one hand, it is strong enough that such series retain certain basic properties of finite sums -- the most important ones being rearrangement of the terms and convergence of products of two infinite series -- that are unfortunately not possessed by all convergent series. On the other hand _____ is weak enough to occur very often in practice.

a. Eisenstein series
b. ACTRAN
c. Alternating series test
d. Absolute convergence

38. For the largest k where $a_k \neq 0$, a_k is called the _____ of P because most often, polynomials are written starting from the left with the largest power of x. So for example the _____ of the polynomial

$$4x^5 + x^3 + 2x^2$$

is 4.

The coefficients of polynomial also may be in the other order:

$$Q(x) = a_0 x^k + a_1 x^{k-1} + \cdots + a_{k-1} x^1 + a_k$$

and must be $a_0 \neq 0$ and a_0 is the _____ of Q.

a. Discriminant
b. Leading coefficient
c. Symmetric function
d. Resultant

39. In mathematics, a _____ is a constant multiplicative factor of a certain object. For example, in the expression $9x^2$, the _____ of x^2 is 9.

The object can be such things as a variable, a vector, a function, etc.

a. Degree of the polynomial
b. Resultant
c. Coefficient
d. Binomial type

40. In mathematics, a _____ is an expression such as

$$x = a_0 + \cfrac{1}{a_1 + \cfrac{1}{a_2 + \cfrac{1}{a_3 + \cfrac{1}{\ddots}}}}$$

where a_0 is an integer and all the other numbers a_i ($i \neq 0$) are positive integers. Longer expressions are defined analogously. If the partial numerators and partial denominators are allowed to assume arbitrary values, which may in some contexts include functions, the resulting expression is a generalized _____.

a. Quadratic equation
b. Restricted partial quotients
c. Stern-Brocot tree
d. Continued fraction

41. In calculus, the _____ determines whether a given critical point of a function is a maximum, a minimum, or neither.

Suppose that f is a function and we want to determine if f has a maximum or minimum at x. If f is increasing to the left of x and decreasing to the right of x, then x is a local maximum of f.

a. Continuous function
b. First derivative test
c. Test for Divergence
d. Partial sum

42. In Geometry, the _____ is an algebraic curve defined by the equation

$$x^3 + y^3 - 3axy = 0$$

It forms a loop in the first quadrant with a double point at the origin and asymptote

$$x + y + a = 0$$

It is symmetrical about y = x.

a. Curve
b. Prolate cycloid
c. Cochleoid
d. Folium of Descartes

Chapter 14. VECTOR CALCULUS

43. In mathematics, _____ and minima, known collectively as extrema, are the largest value (maximum) or smallest value (minimum), that a function takes in a point either within a given neighbourhood (local extremum) or on the function domain in its entirety (global extremum.)

Throughout, a point refers to an input (x), while a value refers to an output (y): one distinguishing between the maximum value and the point (or points) at which it occurs.

A real-valued function f defined on the real line is said to have a local maximum point at the point x^*, if there exists some $\varepsilon > 0$, such that $f(x^*) \geq f(x)$ when $|x - x^*| < \varepsilon$.

a. Related rates
b. Leibniz formula
c. Racetrack principle
d. Maxima

44. _____ is how much exposed area an object has. It is expressed in square units. If an object has flat faces, its _____ can be calculated by adding together the areas of its faces.

a. Plane curve
b. Vector area
c. Lipschitz domain
d. Surface area

45. In mathematics, a _____ is a definite integral taken over a surface (which may be a curved set in space); it can be thought of as the double integral analog of the line integral. Given a surface, one may integrate over it scalar fields (that is, functions which return numbers as values), and vector fields (that is, functions which return vectors as values.)

Surface integrals have applications in physics, particularly with the classical theory of electromagnetism.

a. Contact
b. Symmetry of second derivatives
c. Differential operator
d. Surface integral

46. If a particular point on a sphere is (arbitrarily) designated as its _____, then the corresponding antipodal point is called the south pole and the equator is the great circle that is equidistant to them. Great circles through the two poles are called lines (or meridians) of longitude, and the line connecting the two poles is called the axis of rotation. Circles on the sphere that are parallel to the equator are lines of latitude.

a. Tangent line
b. North pole
c. Sphere
d. Minimal surface

47. In mathematics, the _____, sometimes called the direct _____ is a criterion for convergence or divergence of a series whose terms are real or complex numbers. The test determines convergence by comparing the terms of the series in question with those of a series whose convergence properties are known.

The _____ states that if the series

$$\sum_{n=1}^{\infty} b_n$$

is an absolutely convergent series and

$$|a_n| \leq |b_n|$$

for sufficiently large n , then the series

$$\sum_{n=1}^{\infty} a_n$$

converges absolutely.

a. Conditionally convergent
b. Telescoping series
c. Ratio test
d. Comparison test

48. In mathematics, the concept of a '_____' is used to describe the behavior of a function as its argument or input either 'gets close' to some point, or as the argument becomes arbitrarily large; or the behavior of a sequence's elements as their index increases indefinitely. Limits are used in calculus and other branches of mathematical analysis to define derivatives and continuity.

In formulas, _____ is usually abbreviated as lim

a. BDDC
b. 15 theorem
c. BIBO stability
d. Limit

49. A surface S in the Euclidean space R³ is _____ if a two-dimensional figure (for example,) cannot be moved around the surface and back to where it started so that it looks like its own mirror image (.) Otherwise the surface is non-_____.

More precisely, and applicable to non-embedded surfaces, a surface is non-_____ if there is a continuous map f from the product of a 2-dimensional disk D and the unit interval [0,1] to the surface, $f : D \times [0, 1] \to S$ such that f(c,t) = f(d,t) only if c = d for every t in [0,1], and there exists a reflection map r such that f(d,0) = f(r(d),1) for every d in D.

a. Orientable
b. ACTRAN
c. AUSM
d. ALGOR

50. The _____ is the equation of state of a hypothetical ideal gas, first stated by Benoît Paul Émile Clapeyron in 1834. The law is derived from the fact that in the ideal state of any gas a given number of its 'particles' occupy the same volume, and that volume changes are inverse to pressure changes and linear to temperature changes.

The state of an amount of gas is determined by its pressure, volume, and temperature according to the equation:

$$pV = nRT$$

where

> p is the absolute pressure of the gas,
> V is the volume of the gas,
> n is the number of moles of gas,
> R is the universal gas constant,
> T is the absolute temperature.

a. ALGOR
c. AUSM

b. ACTRAN
d. Ideal gas law

51. The _____ is an important partial differential equation which describes the distribution of heat (or variation in temperature) in a given region over time. For a function u(x,y,z,t) of three spatial variables (x,y,z) and the time variable t, the _____ is

$$\frac{\partial u}{\partial t} - k\left(\frac{\partial^2 u}{\partial x^2} + \frac{\partial^2 u}{\partial y^2} + \frac{\partial^2 u}{\partial z^2}\right) = 0$$

or equivalently

$$\frac{\partial u}{\partial t} = k\nabla^2 u$$

where k is a constant.

The _____ is of fundamental importance in diverse scientific fields.

a. BIBO stability
c. 15 theorem

b. Heat equation
d. BDDC

52. A _____ is a mathematical equation for an unknown function of one or several variables that relates the values of the function itself and of its derivatives of various orders. they play a prominent role in engineering, physics, economics and other disciplines.

A simplified real world example of a _____ is modeling the acceleration of a ball falling through the air (considering only gravity and air resistance.)

a. Structural stability
b. Phase line
c. Differential equation
d. Caloric polynomial

53. For an orientable surface, a consistent choice of 'clockwise' (as opposed to counter-clockwise) is called an orientation, and the surface is called _____. An orientable surface admits exactly 2 orientations, and the distinction between an _____ surface and an orientable surface is subtle and frequently blurred. An orientable surface is an abstract surface that admits an orientation, while an _____ surface is a surface that is abstractly orientable, and has the additional datum of a choice of one of the 2 possible orientations.
   a. ACTRAN
   b. AUSM
   c. ALGOR
   d. Oriented

54. In mathematics and physics, a _____ associates a scalar value, which can be either mathematical in definition to every point in space. Scalar fields are often used in physics, for instance to indicate the temperature distribution throughout space or more specifically, differential geometry, the set of functions defined on a manifold define the commutative ring of functions.
   a. Level curve
   b. Vector Laplacian
   c. Symmetry of second derivatives
   d. Scalar field

55. In mathematics, the _____ is an extension of the factorial function to real and complex numbers. For a complex number z with positive real part the _____ is defined by

$$\Gamma(z) = \int_0^\infty t^{z-1} e^{-t}\, dt \ .$$

This definition can be extended to the rest of the complex plane, excepting the non-positive integers.

If n is a positive integer, then

$\Gamma(n) = (n - 1)!,$

showing the connection to the factorial function.

   a. Gamma function
   b. Digamma function
   c. Pochhammer k-symbol
   d. Multivariate gamma function

56. In vector calculus a conservative vector field is a vector field which is the gradient of a scalar potential. There are two closely related concepts: path independence and _____ vector fields. Every conservative vector field has zero curl (and is thus _____), and every conservative vector field has the path independence property.
   a. AUSM
   b. ACTRAN
   c. ALGOR
   d. Irrotational

57. In physics, and more specifically kinematics, _____ is the change in velocity over time. Because velocity is a vector, it can change in two ways: a change in magnitude and/or a change in direction. In one dimension, _____ is the rate at which something speeds up or slows down.

a. AUSM
b. ALGOR
c. Acceleration
d. ACTRAN

Chapter 1

1. b	2. a	3. a	4. d	5. d	6. b	7. a	8. d	9. d	10. d
11. d	12. d	13. c	14. b	15. c	16. d	17. d	18. d	19. d	20. d
21. b	22. b	23. d	24. b	25. c	26. d	27. c	28. d	29. d	30. b
31. c	32. d	33. d	34. d	35. b	36. d	37. d	38. d	39. c	40. d
41. c	42. d	43. b	44. c	45. c	46. d	47. d	48. d	49. c	50. b
51. d	52. c	53. a	54. d	55. d	56. a	57. d	58. b	59. d	60. c
61. a	62. d	63. a	64. d						

Chapter 2

1. a	2. c	3. a	4. d	5. d	6. b	7. c	8. d	9. d	10. c
11. d	12. a	13. b	14. d	15. c	16. d	17. c	18. d	19. a	20. c
21. a	22. d	23. a	24. d	25. c	26. d	27. c	28. d	29. b	30. a
31. b	32. d	33. c	34. d	35. d	36. b	37. c	38. a	39. d	40. b
41. a	42. c								

Chapter 3

1. a	2. c	3. d	4. d	5. c	6. d	7. d	8. c	9. c	10. a
11. b	12. a	13. b	14. b	15. a	16. d	17. d	18. d	19. d	20. a
21. d	22. d	23. c	24. b	25. d	26. d	27. d	28. d	29. d	30. d
31. a	32. d	33. d	34. c	35. d	36. d	37. d	38. d	39. c	40. d
41. c	42. d	43. d	44. d	45. d	46. c	47. b	48. b	49. d	50. c
51. a	52. d	53. d							

Chapter 4

1. d	2. b	3. d	4. d	5. d	6. d	7. d	8. d	9. d	10. b
11. b	12. d	13. d	14. d	15. d	16. c	17. d	18. a	19. b	20. b
21. d	22. a	23. d	24. d	25. d	26. c	27. d	28. b	29. b	30. d
31. c	32. d	33. c	34. d	35. d	36. d	37. a	38. b	39. d	40. b
41. d	42. d								

Chapter 5

1. d	2. d	3. d	4. d	5. c	6. a	7. a	8. d	9. d	10. d
11. b	12. d	13. d	14. d	15. d	16. d	17. a	18. c	19. c	20. d
21. d	22. d	23. d	24. c	25. d	26. b	27. d	28. d	29. d	30. d
31. d	32. c	33. d	34. d	35. d	36. c	37. b	38. c	39. b	40. d
41. d	42. c	43. d	44. d	45. b	46. d	47. d	48. d		

Chapter 6

1. d	2. a	3. d	4. a	5. d	6. b	7. a	8. b	9. a	10. d
11. a	12. d	13. b	14. b	15. d	16. c	17. d	18. b	19. d	20. c
21. b	22. c	23. a	24. c	25. c	26. d	27. a	28. d	29. c	30. d
31. d	32. d	33. b	34. d	35. a	36. c	37. b	38. d	39. b	40. a
41. a	42. d	43. d	44. d	45. d	46. d	47. a	48. a	49. d	50. b
51. d	52. a								

ANSWER KEY

Chapter 7
1. a 2. b 3. a 4. d 5. d 6. d 7. d 8. d 9. a 10. c
11. d 12. d 13. b 14. b 15. a 16. d 17. c 18. d 19. d 20. d
21. b 22. a

Chapter 8
1. d 2. c 3. d 4. a 5. d 6. c 7. b 8. d 9. d 10. a
11. c 12. d 13. b 14. b 15. d 16. a 17. d 18. d 19. d 20. a
21. a 22. c 23. b 24. d 25. c 26. d 27. a 28. b 29. a 30. d
31. b 32. d 33. b 34. c 35. d 36. d 37. d 38. d 39. d 40. b
41. c 42. d 43. b 44. d 45. d 46. d 47. a 48. b 49. d 50. d
51. a 52. c 53. d 54. a 55. b 56. c

Chapter 9
1. d 2. d 3. d 4. b 5. d 6. d 7. d 8. b 9. d 10. b
11. a 12. d 13. d 14. a 15. d 16. c 17. b 18. d 19. c 20. b
21. c 22. c 23. d 24. d 25. d 26. d 27. b 28. d 29. c 30. d
31. d 32. a 33. c 34. b 35. c

Chapter 10
1. b 2. d 3. d 4. d 5. b 6. d 7. b 8. b 9. c 10. c
11. b 12. a 13. c 14. a 15. d 16. c 17. b 18. d 19. a 20. d
21. d 22. b 23. d 24. a 25. d 26. a 27. a 28. b 29. a 30. c
31. c 32. d 33. d 34. a 35. c 36. a 37. d 38. d 39. d 40. d
41. c 42. b 43. d 44. b 45. d 46. d 47. d 48. d 49. d 50. d
51. c 52. d 53. b 54. a 55. a 56. a 57. a 58. a 59. a 60. d
61. c 62. c 63. d 64. b 65. d 66. c 67. c

Chapter 11
1. c 2. c 3. d 4. c 5. b 6. a 7. b 8. b 9. d 10. a
11. d 12. d 13. a 14. d 15. d 16. a 17. c 18. a 19. d 20. d
21. d 22. c 23. d 24. d 25. a 26. c 27. c 28. a 29. b 30. d
31. d 32. a 33. d 34. d 35. b 36. a 37. d 38. b 39. d 40. a
41. a 42. d 43. a 44. d 45. c 46. b 47. a 48. d 49. d 50. c
51. d 52. d 53. b 54. d 55. b 56. d 57. c 58. b 59. a 60. c
61. a 62. a 63. a 64. a 65. b

Chapter 12
1. d 2. a 3. a 4. d 5. d 6. a 7. c 8. b 9. d 10. a
11. c 12. d 13. b 14. c 15. a 16. b 17. d 18. a 19. d 20. d
21. a 22. a 23. d 24. a 25. c 26. d 27. b 28. b 29. d 30. d
31. d 32. d 33. a 34. d 35. d 36. c 37. d 38. b 39. b 40. b
41. d 42. d 43. a 44. b 45. b 46. a 47. b 48. c 49. d 50. d
51. c 52. a

Chapter 13

1. c	2. b	3. b	4. a	5. b	6. b	7. d	8. a	9. a	10. d
11. a	12. d	13. d	14. d	15. d	16. d	17. a	18. d	19. c	20. a
21. c	22. d	23. d	24. a	25. d	26. d	27. a	28. a	29. b	30. d
31. d	32. c	33. b	34. d	35. d	36. d	37. b	38. d	39. d	

Chapter 14

1. a	2. a	3. d	4. b	5. d	6. d	7. b	8. c	9. a	10. d
11. b	12. d	13. d	14. c	15. d	16. d	17. d	18. d	19. d	20. a
21. d	22. d	23. d	24. c	25. d	26. a	27. b	28. b	29. d	30. d
31. d	32. d	33. d	34. b	35. a	36. c	37. d	38. b	39. c	40. d
41. b	42. d	43. d	44. d	45. d	46. b	47. d	48. d	49. a	50. d
51. b	52. c	53. d	54. d	55. a	56. d	57. c			

www.ingramcontent.com/pod-product-compliance
Lightning Source LLC
Chambersburg PA
CBHW082203230426
43672CB00015B/2884